# Reviewing the Stock
# of Regulation

**OECD**

BETTER POLICIES FOR BETTER LIVES

This document, as well as any data and map included herein, are without prejudice to the status of or sovereignty over any territory, to the delimitation of international frontiers and boundaries and to the name of any territory, city or area.

The statistical data for Israel are supplied by and under the responsibility of the relevant Israeli authorities. The use of such data by the OECD is without prejudice to the status of the Golan Heights, East Jerusalem and Israeli settlements in the West Bank under the terms of international law.

**Please cite this publication as:**
OECD (2020), *Reviewing the Stock of Regulation*, OECD Best Practice Principles for Regulatory Policy, OECD Publishing, Paris, *https://doi.org/10.1787/1a8f33bc-en*.


ISBN 978-92-64-96538-6 (print)
ISBN 978-92-64-69384-5 (pdf)


OECD Best Practice Principles for Regulatory Policy
ISSN 2311-6005 (print)
ISSN 2311-6013 (online)

# Foreword

This report is part of a series of "best practice principles" produced under the auspices of the OECD Regulatory Policy Committee.

The OECD Regulatory Policy Committee is at the forefront of building international consensus on matters of regulatory policy. For almost a decade, the Committee has formally recognised the importance of ensuring that regulations remain fit for purpose over time, and that the best means to achieve this is through *ex post* reviews. That said, the *2012 Recommendation on Regulatory Policy and Governance* provides little advice to governments about the required institutional, analytical, and political arrangements. The purpose of the principles is to fill that void and assist member countries in strengthening existing arrangements, as well as to aid those who are yet to establish a regulatory review system.

This document was approved by the Regulatory Policy Committee at its 21st Session on 6 November 2019 and prepared for publication by the OECD Secretariat.

# Acknowledgements

The principles were prepared by the OECD Public Governance Directorate (GOV), under the leadership of Janos Bertok, Acting Director. They were drafted by Gary Banks, ancillary to his role as Chair of the OECD Regulatory Policy Committee and as a consultant, along with Nick Malyshev, Head of the Regulatory Policy Division and Paul Davidson, Policy Analyst of the Regulatory Policy Division. Jennifer Stein co-ordinated the editorial process.

Thanks are extended to all members of the Regulatory Policy Committee who provided substantial comments and support to the various drafts of the principles. Extensive and useful comments were provided in the public consultation by Steve Glangé, Ministry of Digitalisation, Luxembourg, and Nick Morgan, Better Regulation Executive, Department for Business, Energy and Industrial Strategy, UK.

# Table of contents

## Tables

## Figures

## Boxes

# Abbreviations and acronyms

| BI | Behavioural insights |
| CBA | Cost-benefit analysis |
| RIA | Regulatory impact assessment |
| RIS | Regulation impact statement |
| PC | Productivity Commission (Australia) |
| PIR | Post-implementation review |

# Executive summary

Just as new regulatory proposals need to be assessed to ensure they are fit for purpose and will yield net benefits to society, so, too, do existing regulations, which tend to greatly outnumber new ones and which were often introduced under different circumstances. The *OECD 2012 Recommendation on Regulatory Policy and Governance* states that member countries should "conduct systematic reviews ... to ensure that regulations remain ... cost effective and consistent, and deliver the intended policy objectives".

Despite its importance however, completing the regulatory lifecycle via *ex post* reviews tends to be the "forgotten child" of regulatory policy, with governments often adopting a "set and forget" approach. It is easy to see why this is the case. Proposed regulations often have uncertain impacts, attract media attention, and require political compromise to secure their passage. By contrast, existing laws do not elicit the same interest or sense of urgency as new laws. More importantly though, governments may be fearful a review finds that a regulation has not helped to solve the problem that it was designed to fix. It is hoped that these principles will remind both political and policy leaders that all regulations are experiments, that some experiments fail, and that some experiments require changes before they are successful.

There are three overarching principles that should apply to systems for the *ex post* review of regulation:

- *ex post* reviews should be an integral and permanent part of the regulatory cycle
- review processes should be comprehensive, and
- they should include an evidence-based assessment of the actual outcomes from regulatory action, and contain recommendations to address any deficiencies.

The Best Practice Principles for Reviewing the Stock of Regulation provide advice across the following eight areas within regulatory systems for the *ex post* review of regulation.

The **governance** of *ex post* reviews is key to their effectiveness. Elements of good governance include effective oversight and accountability mechanisms; institutional arrangements that encompass both *ex ante* and *ex post* review processes; and advance notice given to stakeholders of relevant forthcoming reviews.

With respect to the governance of individual reviews, the principle of proportionality should be applied to ensure their cost effectiveness. In addition, while many reviews will be (appropriately) undertaken within the departments responsible, this should not be the case in those agencies tasked with enforcing regulations. The more "sensitive" an area of regulation, and the more significant its impacts, the stronger the case for an arm's length or independent review process. Moreover, the transparency of such reviews is paramount.

A **portfolio of approaches** will generally be needed to ensure that the type of review undertaken is the most suitable and cost-effective. There are three broad review types:

- *Programmed reviews* can include a) reviews for which a requirement is embedded in the legislation itself, especially for more significant and innovative laws; b) sunset requirements for the mass of subordinate regulation; and c) post-implementation reviews conducted within a shorter timeframe as a failsafe mechanism where processes for developing regulation may have been deficient.
- *Ad hoc reviews* encompass "stocktakings" of regulations across a sector or economy, including those screened against criteria such as anti-competitive effects; in-depth public reviews of major regulatory regimes, and the benchmarking of certain regulations where like-for-like comparisons can be made.
- *Ongoing stock management* includes administrative processes that enable learning-by-doing as regulations are implemented; as well as offset rules for new regulations and burden reduction targets (such as various "red tape reduction" initiatives) as a means of reducing the number and cost of existing regulations.

**Essential questions to be answered** in conducting *ex post* reviews are: whether a valid rationale still exists for regulating (appropriateness); whether the regulations achieved their objectives (effectiveness); whether they have given rise to unnecessary costs or other unintended impacts (efficiency), and whether modifications, removal or replacement are called for.

The general **methodology** for conducting evaluations should be within a cost-benefit framework, in which the various impacts of a regulation are identified and documented and their relative magnitudes assessed. Quantification is to be encouraged where feasible as it brings greater rigour to assessments. Moreover, the observed outcomes from regulatory actions ideally should be compared to what could otherwise have occurred in the absence of regulation.

**Consultations** need to be undertaken with affected parties, using processes that are as accessible as possible. The coverage and duration of consultations should be proportionate to the significance of the regulation and its impacts, and the degree of public interest or concern.

**Prioritisation and sequencing** are important to maximise the gains from reforms. Higher priority should be given to reviewing regulations that have a) wide coverage across the economy or society, b) significant impacts on citizens, and for which there is c) *prima facie* evidence of a "problem". There are also benefits in reviewing regulations as a group where they are interactive in nature or operate jointly to meet a policy objective.

**Acquiring in-house capability** in evaluation is essential both for conducting internal reviews and for overseeing work commissioned externally, including the use of consultants. Capacity enhancement within an agency requires training of existing staff as well as specialist recruitment.

**Committed leadership** is fundamental to effective *ex post* review systems, both at the political level, to ensure adequate ongoing support for evaluation, and at senior levels of the bureaucracy to ensure that principles are put into practice.

# Best practice principles

Building on the *OECD 2012 Recommendation on Regulatory Policy and Governance* (OECD, 2012[1]), the following best practice principles have been devised in relation to *ex post* evaluation.

## Overarching principles

- Regulatory policy frameworks should explicitly incorporate *ex post* reviews as an integral and permanent part of the regulatory cycle.
- A sound system for the *ex post* review of regulation would ensure comprehensive coverage of the regulatory stock over time, while "quality controlling" key reviews and monitoring the operations of the system as a whole.
- Reviews should include an evidence-based assessment of the actual outcomes from regulations against their rationales and objectives, note any lessons and make recommendations to address any performance deficiencies.

## System governance

- There need to be oversight and accountability systems within government administrations to ensure that key areas of regulation are not missed and that reviews are conducted appropriately.
- There are benefits in institutional arrangements that combine oversight of the processes for *ex ante* as well as *ex post* evaluation processes, and that do so across the whole-of-government.
- The type of *ex post* review, and its timing or "trigger", are best determined at the time regulations are made.
- Departments and agencies should provide advance notice of forthcoming reviews of regulation (ideally in the form of an annual "forward regulatory review plan").
- There should be explicit provision in agency budgets to cover the costs of reviewing regulations for which they are responsible.

## Broad approaches to reviews

- A "portfolio" of approaches to the *ex post* review of regulation will generally be needed. In broad terms, such approaches range from programmed reviews, to reviews initiated on an *ad hoc* basis, or as part of ongoing "management" processes.

### *"Programmed" reviews*

- For regulations or laws with potentially important impacts on society or the economy, particularly those containing innovative features or where their effectiveness is uncertain, it is desirable to *embed review requirements* in the legislative/regulatory framework itself.
- *Sunset requirements* provide a useful "failsafe" mechanism to ensure the entire stock of subordinate regulation remains fit for purpose over time.
- *Post-implementation reviews* within a shorter timeframe (1 to 2 years) are relevant to situations in which an *ex ante* regulatory assessment was deemed inadequate (by an oversight body for example) or a regulation was introduced despite known deficiencies or downside risks.

### *Ad hoc reviews*

- Public "*stocktakes*" of regulation provide a periodic opportunity to identify current problem areas in specific sectors or the economy as a whole.
- Stocktake-type reviews can also employ a *screening criterion or principle* to focus on specific performance issues or impacts of concern.
- "*In depth*" *public reviews* are appropriate for major regulatory regimes that involve significant complexities or interactions, or that are highly contentious, or both.
- "Benchmarking" of regulation can be a useful mechanism for identifying improvements based on comparisons with jurisdictions having similar policy frameworks and objectives.

### *Ongoing stock management*

- There need to be mechanisms in place that enable "on the ground" learnings within enforcement bodies about a regulation's performance to be conveyed as a matter of course to areas of government with policy responsibility.
- Regulatory offset rules (such as one-in one-out) and Burden Reduction Targets or quotas need to include a requirement that regulations slated for removal, if still "active", first undergo some form of assessment as to their worth.
- Review methods should themselves be reviewed periodically to ensure that they too remain fit for purpose.

## Governance of individual reviews

- The governance and resourcing of reviews, and the approaches employed, need to be proportionate to the nature and significance of the regulations concerned. While needing to be cost-effective, arrangements should be such as to facilitate findings that are sufficiently well supported to be publicly credible.
- For many regulations, evaluations will be best conducted within the departments or ministries having policy responsibility. Enforcement bodies normally should not conduct reviews themselves, but are uniquely placed to offer relevant information and advice and should be closely consulted.
- The more "sensitive" a regulatory area, and the more significant its economic or social impacts, the stronger the case for an "arm's-length" or independent review process. This in turn requires, at a minimum, that those leading a review are not beholden to the agency concerned, and have no perceived conflicts of interest.

- Transparency is paramount for in-depth reviews. Reviews should be publicly announced, with scope for stakeholder input (see *Public consultation*) and the findings/recommendations as well as the government's response made publicly available.

## Key questions to be answered in reviews

- *Appropriateness*: reviews should address as a threshold question whether a valid rationale for regulating still exists.
- *Effectiveness*: reviews should determine whether the regulation (or set of regulations) actually achieves the objectives for which it was introduced.
- *Efficiency*: reviews need to determine whether regulations give rise to unnecessary costs (beyond those needed to achieve the regulatory goal) or other unintended impacts
- *Alternatives*: reviews should consider whether modifications to regulations, or their replacement by alternative policy instruments, are called for.

## Methodologies

- Evaluations should be conducted within a cost-benefit framework that firstly identifies and documents impacts of relevance and then assesses their relative magnitudes.
- Quantification should be encouraged where feasible, as it brings additional rigour to assessments of impacts and potential outcomes.
- Data requirements are best considered at the time a regulation is being made, as part of wider consideration of the type of *ex post* review that would be most appropriate.
- The observed impacts of a regulation should ideally be compared with "counterfactuals" – how things might have turned out otherwise.

## Public consultation

- All reviews should involve consultations with affected parties, and to the extent possible, be accessible to civil society.
- The nature and extent (coverage, duration) of consultations should be proportionate to the significance of the regulations and the degree of public interest or sensitivity entailed.

## Prioritisation and sequencing

- High priority should be given to reviewing regulations that have a) wide coverage across the economy or community and b) potentially significant impacts on citizens or organisations – i.e. "breadth and depth" – and for which there is c) *prima facie* evidence of a "problem".
- Attention to sequencing can be important to maximise the realised gains from reforms.
- There are benefits in reviewing regulations as a group, rather than in a piecemeal fashion, where they are interactive or operate jointly to achieve related policy objectives.

## Capacity building

- Having in-house capability in evaluation and review methods is essential, both in order to conduct reviews internally as well as to oversee those commissioned externally.
- Capacity enhancement needs to be pursued through the training of existing staff as well as through recruitment, with on-the-job learning an important element.
- Consultants can usefully supplement the expertise available within government, but how they may best contribute in specific cases needs careful consideration, and they should not be over utilised to the detriment of internal capability.

## Committed leadership

- Support from political leaders is essential to the establishment and ongoing effectiveness of systems for the *ex post* review of regulation.
- Senior officials within the bureaucracy need to promote a culture of evaluation within their organisations and be vigilant in ensuring that good practice is actually followed "on the ground".

## Reference

OECD (2012), *Recommendation of the Council on Regulatory Policy and Governance*, OECD Publishing, Paris, https://www.oecd.org/governance/regulatory-policy/49990817.pdf. [1]

# Background and context

This is the latest in a series of reports on "best practice principles" produced under the auspices of the OECD Regulatory Policy Committee. As with other reports in the series, it provides an extension and elaboration of principles highlighted in the *OECD 2012 Recommendation of the Council on Regulatory Policy and Governance* (OECD, 2012[1]).

The principles are intended to be relevant and useful to all member governments. They thus offer general guidance rather than providing detailed prescription. Nevertheless, in seeking to invoke "best practice" the principles are intentionally ambitious. Few if any countries could be expected to meet them all. But since they are grounded in the actual experience of different countries, they should not be seen as unattainable or merely aspirational.

## "Evaluation" versus "review"

The literature generally identifies three forms of *ex post* evaluation of regulation (or other policy programmes): those concerned with administration, with compliance and with "outcome performance" (Coglianese, 2012[2]). However the role that *ex post* reviews play in completing and renewing the regulatory cycle, as discussed below, suggests the need for a more holistic interpretation.

*Ex post* assessments of regulatory performance in practice involve a symmetry with *ex ante* assessments: through verifying that stated objectives have actually been met, determining whether there have been any unforeseen or unintended consequences, and considering whether alternative approaches could have done better. This requires clarity about the intended objectives and/or outcomes sought. It also needs data requirements to be embedded such that outcomes can later be measured.

From this perspective, *reviews* can be thought of as conceptually broader than *evaluations*, as they generally encompass proposals for change and may need to revisit the original regulatory objective and its ongoing appropriateness or legitimacy. (For example, an evaluation of a regulation intended to restrict competition may find that it had done that very well, but the approach itself may no longer be accepted as in the public interest.) In other words, while reviews will need to call on evaluation techniques, they have a broader role to play.

The approaches employed for reviews of regulations, like regulations themselves, need to be "fit for purpose". The extent to which this is satisfied can be considered at two levels: first with regard to broad approaches and review mechanisms, and second with regard to the tools or methodologies employed as part of these.

## Why review existing regulations?

The "stock" of regulation is extensive in all countries, typically having accumulated over many years, and its effects across the community and economy can be pervasive. While much of the regulatory stock yields important benefits, its effectiveness will vary and the associated costs can sometimes be greater than is necessary to achieve a policy objective.

The potential for regulation to have significant impacts – whether positive or negative – necessitates it being carefully assessed before implementation. While this is now generally recognised and regulatory impact assessment processes have become increasingly common (OECD, 2015[3]), assessments in the past may not always have been adequate, or undertaken at all.

Even where regulations are rigorously tested before being introduced, not all of their effects can be known with certainty. The regulatory endeavour is essentially experimental in nature, depending to some extent on judgments about causal relationships and responses.

Importantly, regulations that have been properly assessed and well designed, and thus deemed fit for purpose initially, need not remain so. Markets change; technologies advance and preferences, values and behaviours within societies evolve. Moreover, the very accumulation of regulations over time can lead to interactions among them that exacerbate costs or reduce benefits, or have other unintended consequences.

It is also evident that the *stock* of regulations will generally be much larger than the *flow*, with the aggregate impacts commensurately greater. Even a small improvement in the quality of the regulatory stock, therefore, could bring large gains to society.

This is illustrated by the documented instances of cost savings under regulatory burden reduction programs in several OECD countries (OECD, 2011[4]). But there is also considerable potential for other gains from addressing adverse incentive effects on innovation, investment and efficiency. The OECD has analysed the potential gains to member countries from reforms to product and labour market regulations and other structural reforms, finding that convergence to best practice over a five year period would generate sizeable gains for the majority (Bouis and Duval, 2011[5]). To take a specific example, reforms to anti-competitive regulation in Australia during the microeconomic reform programs of the 1980s and 90s were estimated to yield gains totalling some 5% of GDP, with households across all income groups significantly better off (Australian Productivity Commission, 2006[6]).

Evaluations of existing regulations can also yield useful learnings about ways of improving the design and administration of *new* regulations – for example, to reduce compliance costs or change behaviour more effectively. In this way, *ex post* reviews complete the "regulatory cycle" that begins with *ex ante* assessment of proposals and proceeds to implementation and administration (OECD, 2015[3]).

Importantly, the knowledge that new regulatory initiatives will be reviewed can engender greater public support for them (or weaken opposition) and may enhance trust in government itself. Trust is likely to be further increased by inclusive review processes that draw on views and evidence from stakeholders and the public (Lind and Arndt, 2016[7]).

## Why a need for "*principles*"?

The importance of using *ex post* reviews to assess the ongoing worth of regulations is recognised in the *OECD 2012 Recommendation on Regulatory Policy and Governance* (OECD, 2012[1]). It states that member governments should:

> *Conduct systematic reviews of the stock of regulation ... to ensure that regulations remain up to date, ... cost effective and consistent, and deliver the intended policy objectives.*

Based on the Indicators of Regulatory Policy and Governance surveys, systems for the *ex post* review of regulation remain less developed than for other components of the regulatory cycle, particularly *ex ante* assessments, with fewer countries having formalised arrangements. For example, some form of *ex post* evaluation was recorded as obligatory by only 60% of member countries, compared to around 90% for *ex ante* assessment (OECD, 2015[3]), (OECD, 2018[8]). There was little improvement between the two surveys, apart from a rise in the use of stock/flow linkage rules (Figure 1).

## Figure 1. Requirements to conduct RIA and *ex post* evaluation

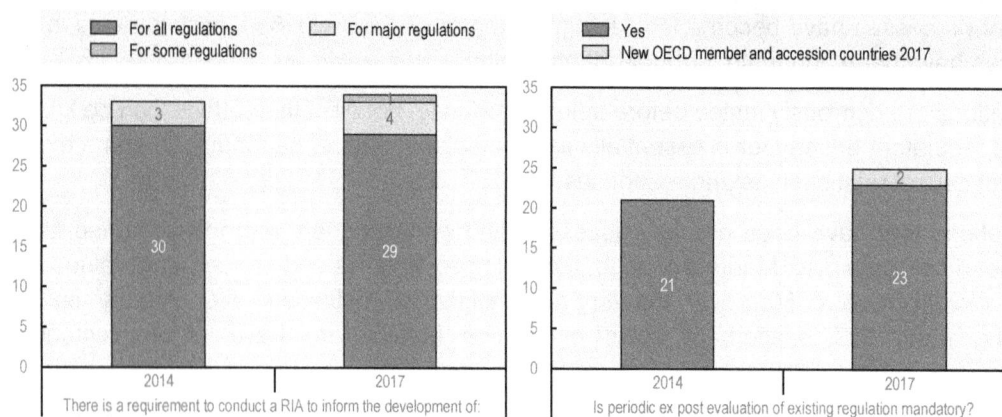

Notes: Data for OECD countries is based on the 34 countries that were OECD members in 2014 and the European Union. Data on new OECD member and accession countries 2017 includes Colombia, Costa Rica, Latvia and Lithuania.
Source: Indicators of Regulatory Policy and Governance Surveys 2014 and 2017, http://oe.cd/ireg.

The reality is that *ex post* assessments of regulations are in some respects more demanding and less straightforward than assessments undertaken at the proposals stage. This reflects in part the challenges posed by the large number of regulations potentially involved, and a need for different approaches and methods in different contexts.

There will typically also be more political or bureaucratic resistance to scrutiny of regulations in place than for those in prospect. This is understandable, in light of the possibility of a review finding that certain regulations introduced previously have been unduly costly or failed to achieve their objectives.

Given the weaker incentives for *ex post* than for *ex ante* assessments, it is useful to have systems in place to ensure that reviews are conducted. The following principles should assist in guiding improvements in the areas where this is needed.

## References

Australian Productivity Commission (2006), *Potential Benefits of the National Reform Agenda,*   [6]
*Report to the Council of Australian Governments,*
https://www.pc.gov.au/research/completed/national-reform-agenda/nationalreformagenda.pdf
(accessed on 2 July 2020).

Bouis, R. and R. Duval (2011), "Raising Potential Growth After the Crisis: A Quantitative   [5]
Assessment of the Potential Gains from Various Structural Reforms in the OECD Area and
Beyond", *OECD Economics Department Working Papers*, No. 835, OECD Publishing, Paris,
https://dx.doi.org/10.1787/5kgk9qj18s8n-en.

Coglianese, C. (2012), *Measuring Regulatory Performance: Evaluating the Impact of Regulation*   [2]
*and Regulatory Policy*, http://www.oecd.org/gov/regulatory-policy/1_coglianese%20web.pdf.

Lind, E. and C. Arndt (2016), "Perceived Fairness and Regulatory Policy: A Behavioural Science   [7]
Perspective on Government-Citizen Interactions", *OECD Regulatory Policy Working Papers*,
No. 6, OECD Publishing, Paris, https://dx.doi.org/10.1787/1629d397-en.

OECD (2018), *OECD Regulatory Policy Outlook 2018*, OECD Publishing, Paris, [8]
https://dx.doi.org/10.1787/9789264303072-en.

OECD (2015), *OECD Regulatory Policy Outlook 2015*, OECD Publishing, Paris, [3]
https://dx.doi.org/10.1787/9789264238770-en.

OECD (2012), *Recommendation of the Council on Regulatory Policy and Governance*, OECD [1]
Publishing, Paris, https://dx.doi.org/10.1787/9789264209022-en.

OECD (2011), *Regulatory Policy and Governance: Supporting Economic Growth and Serving* [4]
*the Public Interest*, OECD Publishing, Paris, https://dx.doi.org/10.1787/9789264116573-en.

# 1 Overarching principles

Consistent with the *OECD 2012 Recommendation on Regulatory Policy and Governance* (OECD, 2012[1]), there are three high level principles that should have wide applicability, regardless of the institutional settings of individual countries.

## Regulatory policy frameworks should explicitly incorporate *ex post* reviews as an integral and permanent part of the regulatory cycle.

The broadly accepted notion of a "regulatory cycle" recognises that regulations are akin potentially to depreciating assets that require ongoing management and renewal. For reasons just noted, even if they start out well, many regulations may no longer be fit for purpose some years hence. The accumulated costs of this in economic or social terms can be high.

It is fundamental to achieving and sustaining good regulatory outcomes over time, therefore, that regulatory policy systems explicitly incorporate provision for *ex post* review along with *ex ante* assessment, and requirements for implementation and enforcement. Where such an integrated approach to *ex post* reviews is not in place, governments have the opportunity to pursue this as part of a longer term strategy to improve the overall quality of regulation and thereby bring additional benefits to citizens.

Such requirements can in time also help foster a deeper "culture of evaluation" within government, enhancing administrative capability in this area and raising the standard of evaluations themselves. In so doing, it can also help build (or restore) public trust in government's regulatory role.

## A sound system for the *ex post* reviews of regulation would ensure comprehensive coverage of the regulatory stock over time, while "quality controlling" key reviews and monitoring the operations of the system as a whole.

The stock of regulation remains extensive in all countries, notwithstanding regulatory reforms and red tape reduction programs in many. It is important that opportunities for improving a country's overall regulatory performance are not missed through oversight or neglect (or resistance). How well reviews are conducted can vary, so a strong system would also have the capacity to guide and monitor review processes. And because such systems themselves normally involve a degree of "learning by doing", provision for periodically evaluating their overall performance is also needed (see (OECD, 2010[2]), Annex 2), which investigates the broad benefits from administrative burden reduction programmes and develops a possible methodological framework that could be used for evaluating programmes).

## Reviews should include an evidence-based assessment of the actual outcomes from regulations, against their rationales and objectives; they should note any lessons and make recommendations to address any performance deficiencies.

Just as *ex ante* regulatory impact assessment (RIA) processes seek to determine the likely net benefits of a new regulatory initiative, whether in social or economic terms (or both), *ex post* reviews ideally need to determine the extent to which these have been realised in practice. That would normally include an evaluation not only of compliance costs, but also other costs and benefits that relate to the primary objective of the regulation (e.g. financial stability, harm minimisation, competition, etc.) (Box 1.1). It also means that the financing of any data collection and any subsequent review should be included as part of the costs of the regulatory proposal.

To be useful to policy makers and the public, therefore, it is important that, where needed, *ex post* reviews draw lessons from past experience and contain recommendations for improvement. These could range from minor amendments to the regulations under review, to their removal or replacement. In turn, this feeds back into (re)design processes, highlighting the need for increased resilience and adaptability of regulatory systems, particularly in the face of rapid technological and environmental changes.

---

### Box 1.1. Examples of *ex post* reviews in OECD countries

- A review of the regulatory framework for resource development in Canada found that investors could be discouraged by complex rules and processes, threatening the economic viability of major projects. The Ministry of Finance recommended the implementation of the Responsible Resource Development Plan, which included more predictable project reviews, reduced duplication of review processes, strengthened environmental protection, and enhanced consultation with Aboriginal people.

- The Chilean Productivity Commission undertook a review of its copper mining industry. It made a total of 53 recommendations, a number of which specifically related to the copper mining regulatory environment. It recommended that approval processes for large projects be shortened, to ideally not exceed three years. To achieve this, better coordination within and between government agencies would be required. Further recommendations related to improving the industry's safety and reforming exploration and licencing arrangements.

- The Prime Minister's Office in Finland published a study on investigating the evaluation and reduction of regulatory burdens. The 2018 study concluded that it could not provide an overall assessment of the regulatory burden due to insufficient information from either budget papers (a "top down" approach) or on a law-by-law basis (a "bottoms up" approach). However the report presented 15 proposals to reduce or avoid regulatory burdens, including recommendations on implementation and legislative drafting.

- The German Finance Ministry conducted an in-depth review in 2017 on standard tax forms for citizens. In its conclusions, the Ministry issued recommendations for simplifying tax forms. Following the review, consultation and co-ordination discussions were held with authorities at the subnational level in order to implement the recommendations.

- In 2015, the Israeli Government announced a five-year plan for the reduction of regulatory burdens. In 2016 some 31 different regulatory areas were reviewed, including laws relating to competition, administrative burdens, compliance costs, compliance with international instruments, risk, and regulatory overlap. For example, the Ministry of Environmental Protection examined the regulatory process in the field of integrated licensing of industries, such as non-ionising radiation and hazardous waste. The Ministry expects ILS 74.5 million in annual savings to the economy by reducing interactions with authorities and creating certainty throughout the life of the licence.

- In 2014, an administrative burden review in the United States examined the response of agencies to Executive Order 13610, Identifying and Reducing Regulatory Burdens. In the first iteration of periodic reports implementing the Executive Order, Executive Departments and Agencies identified more than 100 initiatives producing an estimated annual reduction in paperwork burden of more than 100 million hours.

Source: (OECD, 2018[3]); (Comisión Nacional de Productividad, 2017[4]); (Prime Minister's Office: Government Research Activities (Finland), 2018[5]); (Ministry of Finance (Germany), 2020[6]); (Prime Minister's Office: Better Regulation Unit (Israel), 2017[7]); (Office of Management and Budget: Office of Information and Regulatory Affairs (United States), 2016[8]).

---

**There need to be oversight and accountability systems within government administrations to provide ongoing assurance that significant areas of regulation will not be missed and that reviews are conducted appropriately.**

If regulatory agencies and their ministries are left entirely to their own devices, there is a risk that important areas of regulation will not be reviewed, or that reviews will sometimes occur too late (in response to a mishap or "crisis") or that they will not be conducted sufficiently well to inform decisions about the retention or amendment of the regulations concerned. The move to impose RIA requirements within most OECD governments is recognition of this reality.

The functions of such oversight bodies include providing advice about the regulatory assessment obligations of relevant departments and ministries, as well as monitoring compliance. Such bodies will generally also be well-placed to provide or arrange training in review processes and methods for departmental officials.

**There are benefits in institutional arrangements that combine oversight of the processes for *ex ante* as well as *ex post* assessment, and that do so across the whole of government.**

The fact that regulations undergo a number of phases following their initial development argues for oversight and accountability mechanisms that encompass the whole of the "regulatory cycle". In particular, there is a connection between *ex ante* and *ex post* evaluations, with the former setting up the latter and *ex post* reviews being conducted in the light of *ex ante* assessments, as well as helping to inform further evaluations of new or amended regulation (Box 1.2).

---

**Box 1.2. Examples linking *ex ante* and *ex post* regulatory oversight in OECD member countries**

- **Austria** has established the system of "*Wirkungsorientierte Folgenabschätzung*", which introduces systematic requirements for both *ex ante* and *ex post* assessments, and requires major regulations to be evaluated after five years. The Federal Performance Management Office is responsible for ensuring the quality of both *ex ante* and *ex post* assessments. In its 2017 report, a regulatory proposal relating to Funding Alpine Infrastructure was highlighted as it explicitly stated that in order to assess the regulation's actual success, impact-oriented data would be required that would allow for progress to be accurately measured. The evidence base would then be expected to form the basis of the *ex post* evaluation when the regulation was due for review.

- The Regulatory Scrutiny Board of the **European Commission** conducts reviews of *ex ante* impact assessments, as well as selected *ex post* evaluations. Its 2017 annual report analysed how impact assessments and *ex post* evaluations were assessed when regulatory proposals were subject to an informal "upstream meeting" early in the review process with staff of the Commission's services. It generally found that the final impact assessment result had improved where upstream meetings took place – which also tended to be in more complex regulatory areas. The same could not be said for *ex post* evaluations and it was queried whether the limited impact was due to the upstream meeting taking place too late in the evaluation process.

Source: (Austrian Bundesministerium für Öffentlichen Dienst und Sport, 2018[9]); (Regulatory Scrutiny Board (European Commission), 2018[10]).

---

This dual oversight role should ideally be located in a dedicated unit within a single ministry or agency that has a government-wide purview. This is likely to provide greater scope for consistency, skill development, relationship building, and the retention of relevant institutional knowledge. Examples include the oversight bodies from Finland, Mexico, the United Kingdom, and the European Union (Table 1.1).[1]

### Table 1.1. Bodies responsible for overseeing both *ex ante* impact assessment and *ex post* evaluation

| OECD member country | Name of oversight body |
| --- | --- |
| Australia | Office of Best Practice Regulation (OBPR) |
| Austria | Federal Performance Management Office (Federal Chancellery) |
| Austria | Ministry of Finance |
| Denmark | The Inter-Ministerial EU Implementation Committee |
| Estonia | Shared responsibility between Legislative Quality Division, Legislative Policy Department, Ministry of Justice |
| European Commission | Regulatory Scrutiny Board (RSB) |
| European Commission | Secretary General (SG) |
| Finland | Finnish Council of Regulatory Impact Analysis |
| Germany | Better Regulation Unit, Federal Chancellery |
| Greece | Better Regulation Office of the General Secretariat of the Government |
| Israel | Better Regulation Division in the Office of the Prime Minister |
| Italy | Department of legal and legislative affairs (DAGL) of the Presidency of the Council of Ministers |
| Italy | Impact Assessment Independent Unit |
| Japan | Administrative Evaluation Bureau in the Ministry of Internal Affairs and communications |
| Korea | Korea Development Institute (Regulatory Research Center) |
| Korea | Korea Institute of Public Administration (Regulatory Research Center) |
| Korea | Regulatory Reform Committee (RRC) |
| Luxembourg | Ministry of the Civil Service and Administrative Reform |
| Mexico | National Commission for Regulatory Improvement (CONAMER) |
| Poland | Shared responsibility between Government Programming Board supported by Regulatory Impact Assessment Department within the Chancellery of the Prime Minister |
| Poland | Regulatory Risk Assessment Department in the Ministry of Economic Development |
| Spain | Oficina de Coordinación y Calidad Normativa |
| United Kingdom | Regulatory Policy Committee (RPC) |
| United States | Office of Information and Regulatory Affairs |

Note: The table is based on information available for 70 bodies reported in the survey which are responsible for quality control of regulatory management tools.
Source: Survey questions on regulatory oversight bodies, Indicators of Regulatory Policy and Governance Survey 2017, http://oe.cd/ireg.

## The type of *ex post* review, and its timing or "triggers", are generally best determined at the time regulations are being made.

At the stage when regulations are being developed, there would generally be a clearer appreciation of the sort of review that would be most appropriate, given the nature of the regulation, its context and any potential uncertainties about its effects. There is the further advantage that at this point relevant expertise is more likely to be on hand. This approach also enables early consideration of data needs and provision for their collection, which can play a crucial role.

---

[1] The 2015 and 2018 Regulatory Policy Outlooks (OECD, 2015[11]), (OECD, 2018[3]) highlight the emergence in the past ten years of bodies established at arm's length from government and tasked with the scrutiny of regulatory management tools, most notably RIA, and to a lesser extent, *ex post* evaluation.

It follows that it would be desirable for it to be a requirement of *ex ante* assessments that the question of *ex post* reviews be addressed, and an appropriate review type specified in the regulation impact statement (RIS) or other documentation.

## Departments and agencies should provide advance notice of forthcoming reviews of regulation (ideally in the form of an annual "forward regulatory review plan").

Reviews of regulation are often critically dependent on the extent and quality of inputs from those affected by or interested in the regulations concerned. Such inputs are needed both for assessing impacts and outcomes, and also to promote acceptance and support for any regulatory changes that may result. Stakeholder preparation for a review can require considerable data gathering and analysis, which takes time and resources. Adequate notice can facilitate stakeholder preparation. And information relating to other scheduled reviews can help stakeholders prioritise their efforts and more generally help avoid "review fatigue". Forward regulatory planning is becoming more commonplace across the OECD membership, although only around one-third of member countries currently do so for subordinate regulations (Figure 1.1).

### Figure 1.1. Online lists used in regulatory forward planning

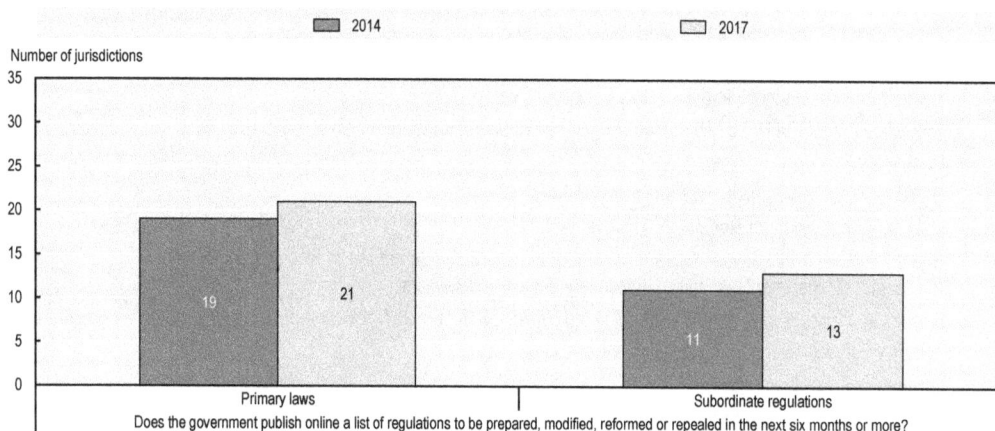

Note: Data is based on 34 OECD member countries and the European Union.
Source: Indicators of Regulatory Policy and Governance Surveys 2014 and 2017, http://oe.cd/ireg.

## There should be explicit provision in agency budgets to cover the costs of reviewing the regulations for which they have responsibility.

Under constrained budgets, *ex post* reviews of regulation can be displaced by activities seen as being more urgent and important at the time. Without explicit provision for the resourcing of reviews, they may either be deferred or avoided, or undertaken in a form inadequate for the purpose (for example, with limited consultation). Reviews need to be seen as an integral part of a department or agency's regulatory functions, rather than an "extra" and this is more likely to be the case with dedicated resourcing.

# References

Austrian Bundesministerium für Öffentlichen Dienst und Sport (2018), *Bericht über die wirkungsorientierte Folgenabschätzung: Bericht gemäß § 68 Abs. 5, BHG 2013 iVm § 6, Wirkungscontrollingverordnung*, https://www.oeffentlicherdienst.gv.at/wirkungsorientierte_verwaltung/dokumente/WFA-Bericht_2017_WEB_2.pdf?6wd8ir. [9]

Comisión Nacional de Productividad (2017), *Productivity in the Chilean Copper Mining Industry*, http://www.comisiondeproductividad.cl/wp-content/uploads/2018/09/Productivity_copper.pdf. [4]

Ministry of Finance (Germany) (2020), *Simplifying tax declarations*, https://www.bundesregierung.de/breg-en/issues/wirksam-regieren-with-citizens-for-citizens/topics/simplifying-tax-declarations-392142. [6]

OECD (2018), *OECD Regulatory Policy Outlook 2018*, OECD Publishing, Paris, https://dx.doi.org/10.1787/9789264303072-en. [3]

OECD (2015), *OECD Regulatory Policy Outlook 2015*, OECD Publishing, Paris, https://dx.doi.org/10.1787/9789264238770-en. [11]

OECD (2012), *Recommendation of the Council on Regulatory Policy and Governance*, OECD Publishing, Paris, https://dx.doi.org/10.1787/9789264209022-en. [1]

OECD (2010), *Why Is Administrative Simplification So Complicated?: Looking beyond 2010*, Cutting Red Tape, OECD Publishing, Paris, https://dx.doi.org/10.1787/9789264089754-en. [2]

Office of Management and Budget: Office of Information and Regulatory Affairs (United States) (2016), *Information Collection Budget of the United States Government*, http://www.whitehouse.gov/omb/inforeg_infocoll/. [8]

Prime Minister's Office: Better Regulation Unit (Israel) (2017), *Regulatory Burden Reduction Summary 2016*, http://185.70.251.162/uploads/reports/7/Regulation2016_ENG2.pdf. [7]

Prime Minister's Office: Government Research Activities (Finland) (2018), *Julkaisija ja julkaisuaika Valtioneuvoston kanslia (Evaluation and reduction of regulatory burden)*, https://tietokayttoon.fi/documents/10616/6354562/27-2018-S%C3%A4%C3%A4ntelytaakan+arviointi+ja+v%C3%A4hent%C3%A4minen.pdf/f32dc48f-4dcf-4088-b7fe-67d50f3b23ac?version=1.0. [5]

Regulatory Scrutiny Board (European Commission) (2018), *Annual Report 2017*, https://ec.europa.eu/info/sites/info/files/rsb-report-2017_en.pdf. [10]

# 2 Broad approaches to reviews

A "portfolio" of approaches to the *ex post* review of regulation will generally be needed. In broad terms, such approaches range from programmed reviews, to reviews initiated on an ad hoc basis, or as part of ongoing "management" processes.

Most countries have adopted more than one of these approaches (OECD, 2015[1]) utilising forms of review within each category listed below (Table 2.1). These draw on a taxonomy developed by the Australian Productivity Commission.

Table 2.1. Approaches and mechanisms for *ex post* reviews of regulation

| Programmed reviews | Ad hoc reviews | Ongoing "management" |
|---|---|---|
| • Sunsetting rules | • Public stocktakes | • Stock-flow linkage rules |
| • Embedded in statute | • Principles-based reviews | • Quantitative red tape reduction targets |
| • Other post-implementation reviews | • In-depth reviews | |
| | • Benchmarking | |

Source: Adapted from (Australian Productivity Commission, 2011[2]).

## "Programmed" reviews

As noted, there are significant benefits in specifying and scheduling reviews well in advance of when they would need to take place. This can be put into effect through different mechanisms.

For regulations or laws with potentially important impacts on society or the economy, particularly those containing innovative features or where their effectiveness is uncertain, it is desirable to embed review requirements in the legislative/regulatory framework itself.

In such cases, a review can be crucial to necessary "learning by doing", as well as for ensuring that there have been no unintended consequences. Embedding a review in the enabling legislation means that the review is more likely to take place when needed and address the key issues of concern. Importantly, it also provides a public signal of the government's desire to achieve good outcomes. An example that could be cited from Australia relates to regulations for third party access to essential economic infrastructure, where the initial legislation made explicit provision for a review within five years, following which review a number of significant design changes were made (Australian Productivity Commission, 2005[3]).

The majority of OECD countries exhibit at least some embedded review requirements, although they are more commonplace in Hungary, Korea, and the United Kingdom (see Box 2.1).

---

**Box 2.1. Examples of embedded review requirements**

- Hungary's RIA guidance material provides that in the development of regulatory proposals, all proposals indicate whether it is necessary for an *ex post* evaluation to be defined in the legislative act. This indicates on a case-by-case basis whether an *ex post* evaluation will take place, and if so when it is expected.

- Pursuant to Article 8 of the Framework Act on Administrative Regulations, all new and amending Acts and subordinate statutes in Korea must provide for an effective review period, which in general should not exceed five years.

- In the United Kingdom, a statutory review is required of all subordinate regulations where those regulations affect either business or a voluntary or community body. The report must set out the objectives to be achieved, assess the extent to which they have been achieved, assess whether those objectives remain appropriate, and if they remain appropriate – assess the extent to which they could be achieved in a less onerous manner. The first report is due within five years of the commencement of the subordinate regulation, with subsequent reviews to be conducted within the next five years.

Source: (OECD, 2018[4]); (Hungarian Administrative and Justice Ministry, n.d.[5]); (Legislation.co.uk, 2015[6]) Sections 28-32.

---

## Sunset requirements provide a useful "failsafe" mechanism to ensure the stock of subordinate regulation remains fit for purpose over time.

"Sunsetting" refers to the automatic lapsing of regulations after a prescribed period unless they have been re-made. Depending on the details of their design and implementation, sunset clauses can be effective in removing regulations that have become redundant or are no longer cost effective, while providing an opportunity to make a case for renewal or modification.

This approach is normally reserved for secondary or subordinate regulations rather than primary legislation, for which the cost and disruption caused by any rules being inadvertently terminated could be high. A number of jurisdictions have separate provisions designed to ensure that other regulations are reviewed within prescribed periods (Box 2.2).

---

**Box 2.2. A summary of sunsetting arrangements in OECD countries**

The latest data indicate that just under half of OECD member countries have some form a sunsetting arrangements in place, and that sunsetting arrangements are more prevalent for subordinate regulations than for primary laws (OECD, 2018[4]). However, for the majority of countries that have sunsetting arrangements, they are generally undertaken on a case by-case basis.

More standardised sunsetting arrangements exist in: France, Germany and Korea (3 to 5 years for both primary laws and subordinate regulations), Mexico (5 years for technical standards relating to subordinate regulations), United Kingdom (no later than 7 years, with a review after 5 years relating to subordinate regulations) and Australia (10 years relating to subordinate regulations). Korea's sunsetting arrangements mirror those of its general review requirements (see above).

Source: (OECD, 2018[4]); (OECD/KDI, 2017[7]).

---

As a failsafe mechanism, sunset clauses normally come into force only after an extended period from when a regulation was made, such as 5-10 years. The rules can be structured for extensive coverage of the regulatory stock, but may also be selective or involve specific carve-outs. Because of the potentially large number of regulations affected, processes need to be managed well to avoid review overload. For example, a recent OECD review of Korea's regulatory governance found that given the amount of regulations due to sunset, review staff in the Prime Minister's Office had just over one day on average to review each sunsetting regulation. Likewise, they need to be done with care to ensure regulatory certainty, especially if carried out close to the "expiration" date.

**Post-implementation reviews within shorter timeframes (1-2 years) are relevant to situations in which either an emergency regulatory measure was deemed necessary, *ex ante* regulatory assessment was judged inadequate, or a regulation proceeded despite known deficiencies or downside risks.**

Post-implementation reviews constitute a further, more targeted "failsafe" designed to detect any unintended adverse impacts in a timely way, before their costs become too great (Box 2.3). They are designed to take place only in exceptional circumstances. Experience suggests that such impacts are more likely in circumstances where *ex ante* processes have been deficient or overridden.

---

### Box 2.3. Post-implementation review requirements

OECD data indicate that eight member countries currently have post implementation review requirements in place: **Australia**, **Hungary**, **Ireland**, **Italy**, **Japan**, **Korea**, **New Zealand** and **Slovenia** (OECD, 2018[4]).

- In **Australia**, there is a general requirement to conduct a review within five years for all new regulations with "a substantial or widespread economic impact". In addition a post-implementation review (PIR) must be conducted within two years for any regulation introduced, removed or significantly changed without an adequate regulation impact statement, including where the Prime Minister has granted an exemption from regulatory impact statement (RIS) requirements because of exceptional circumstances. The Office of Best Practice Regulation maintains a public register of outstanding PIRs and determines whether agencies are complying with best practice.

- In **Slovenia**, where a Bill has been presented to the National Assembly without impact assessment and is adopted by an urgent procedure, a report must be completed sometime after two years from the date of implementation. The report must contain an impact assessment in the same areas as for a standard impact assessment, and the report is then forwarded to the National Assembly for information and published on the government website.

- If special grounds exist for the immediate establishment of a new (or amending) regulation in **Korea**, the head of the proposing ministry can ask the Regulatory Reform Committee to make an emergency decision. Where the Committee decides that a regulation is urgent, it reviews whether the regulation's establishment is reasonable in a 20-day period, and informs the proposing ministry of its findings. The head of the proposing ministry is then required to submit a regulatory impact analysis report within 60 days of the Committee's findings.

Source: OECD (2017); (Australian Office of Best Practice Regulation, 2016[8]); (PISG Legal Information System, n.d.[9]); Framework Act on Administrative Regulations 2013 (Korea).

---

A need to "regulate first" will often arise in crisis situations, where action is called for but there is little time to follow normal procedures. It may also reflect a political judgment that there is value in regulating notwithstanding a technical assessment to the contrary. While these can be legitimate reasons for proceeding to regulate, the reality that risks will generally be greater in such circumstances warrants a review taking place earlier than otherwise would be the case under a more systematic process.

## Ad hoc special purpose reviews

Reviews often need to be initiated on an *ad hoc* basis in response to an emergent issue or crisis, such as a natural disaster or major public health problem. They can also be established to address a more general theme or concern, such as impediments to competition, or to focus on a particular economic activity or segment of society, such as regional development.

Public "stocktakes" of regulation provide a periodic opportunity to identify current problem areas in specific sectors or for the economy as a whole.

"Stocktake" reviews are useful for soliciting public views about current problems and priorities. They can also be an effective means of identifying cumulative regulatory burdens or detecting adverse interactions across different regulations (Figure 2.1).

Given their breadth of coverage and resourcing needs, stocktake reviews should normally only be undertaken at infrequent intervals, say 5 to 10 yearly. And, being complaint driven, they need to be accompanied by robust vetting processes prior to any recommendations being made. For example, in Australia, the Prime Minister's 2005 Regulation Taskforce adopted an approach of initially screening proposals and passing those with apparent merit to the relevant government department for comment before deciding on a recommendation (Regulation Taskforce, 2006[10]).

### Figure 2.1. *Ad hoc* reviews of the stock of regulation conducted in the last 12 years

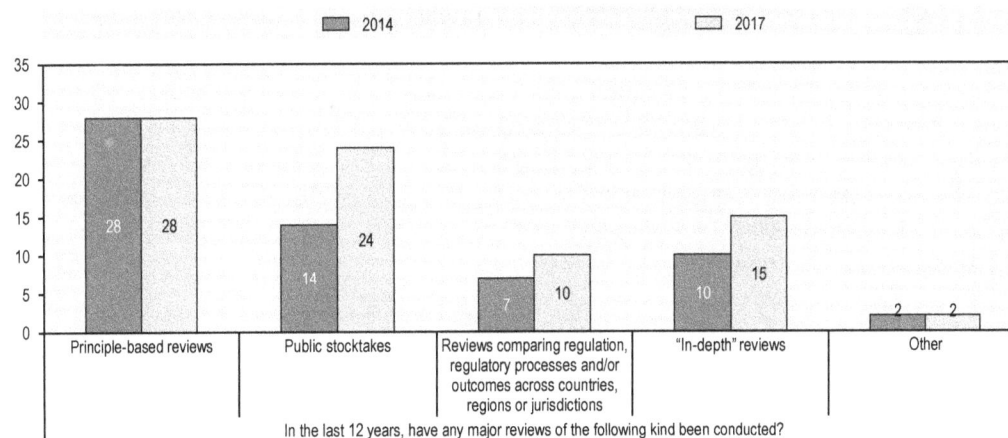

Note: Data is based on 34 OECD member countries and the European Union.
Source: Indicators of Regulatory Policy and Governance Surveys 2014 and 2017, http://oe.cd/ireg

## Stocktake-type reviews can also employ a uniform screening criterion or principle to focus on specific performance issues or impacts of concern.

Such an approach, being more selective, tends to be more manageable than general stocktakes and can enable deeper analysis (Box 2.4). Most countries have conducted such reviews at some point over the past 12 years, based on survey data (shown in chart above). The most common areas of focus have been anti-competitive effects or high compliance burdens (OECD, 2015[11]); OECD 2018).

---

### Box 2.4. Selected principle-based reviews in OECD countries

- In **Australia**, as part of a wider "national competition policy" agreement among Commonwealth, State and Territory Governments, reviews of legislation with identified anti-competitive effects were conducted in the period 1995 to 2005. A new decision rule was instituted that such regulations could only be retained where it could be demonstrated that a) they yielded net benefits to society that outweighed the costs and b) that the policy objectives could only be achieved by impeding competition. Around 80% of some 2 000 individual legislative items were reviewed over the period, with a majority being removed or reformed. This enabled the jurisdiction in those cases to qualify for "competition payments" from the federal government.

- The **Danish** Business Forum for Better Regulation was launched in 2012. It aims to ensure the renewal of business regulation in close dialogue with the business community by identifying areas that businesses perceive as the most burdensome, and to propose simplification measures. For instance, this could include changing rules, or shortening processing times. Thirteen themes are currently covered, ranging from the employment of foreign workers to barriers for growth. Interested parties can submit additional themes. Proposals from the Business Forum are subject to a "comply or explain" principle, whereby the government is required to commit to either implement the proposed initiatives or to justify why the initiatives will not be implemented. As of October 2016, 603 proposals were sent to Government, of which so far 191 were fully and 189 partially implemented. The accumulated annual burden reduction of some initiatives has been estimated at 790 million Danish crowns.

- **Italy's** Simplification Office in the Department of Public Administration recently published a monitoring update to its simplification agenda. The agenda identified five strategic sectors, all of which were fundamental to daily life: digital citizenship; welfare; e-health; tax; and building and business. For instance, the topic relating to digital citizenship has the goal of ensuring increasing online delivery of services and access to communications via the internet. It has subsequently reviewed the following areas: dissemination of the public digital identity system; completion of the national population registry; computerisation of the civil, penal, and administrative processes; the electronic payments system; and average payment times by public administrations.

- Between 2015 and 2017, **Sweden** conducted a review of its hospitality sector, with a particular focus on administrative burden in restaurant permit regulation. The report identified a need to provide guidance for businesses on how to find, understand and coordinate the relevant permits needed to start a restaurant. Consequently, a guide and a checklist tool for setting up a restaurant were launched in May 2016. In 2017, a standardisation project was launched in the form of an e-service on local government websites.

Source: OECD (2017); (OECD, 2016[12]); (Australian Productivity Commission, 2005[3]); (Danish Business Forum, n.d.[13]); (Department of Public Administration Simplification Office (Italy), 2017[14]).

---

## "In-depth" public reviews are appropriate for major regulatory regimes that involve significant complexities or interactions, or that are highly contentious, or both.

In-depth public reviews are characterised by a robust analytical and evidentiary approach. They also need to provide ample scope for stakeholders and the wider public to offer views and provide feedback, especially on any preliminary findings and recommendations.

This makes them a relatively resource-intensive approach, typically requiring considerably more time to complete than other review types. For example, the average duration of public inquiries on high profile regulatory topics conducted by the Productivity Commissions in Australia, Chile and New Zealand has been around 12 months.

It follows that such reviews would normally be reserved for regulatory areas that are of major importance, where there may be a range of regulations and other policy instruments at work, the combined effects of which would need to be understood and accounted for in proposing specific reforms. Nearly half of the OECD membership indicated that it had undertaken an in-depth review between 2014 and 2017 (see, for example, Box 2.5).

---

### Box 2.5. Selected in-depth reviews in OECD countries

- Australia's Productivity Commission (PC) conducts public inquiries into key policy issues referred to it by the federal government, many of which have contained a significant regulatory component alongside other instruments. These include areas of social and environmental as well as economic regulation. For example, the PC has conducted two major reviews of the gambling industries in Australia, the scale and reach of which have expanded greatly following deregulatory initiatives by state governments. It found that the regulatory framework did not take sufficient account of the social costs and policy had been too focused on revenue from tourism and taxation. Recommendations were made in a variety of areas, including regulations constraining spending and loss rates on "electronic gaming machines" and in relation to access to gambling venues and support for "problem gamblers".

- The French Court of Auditors conducted a review of social housing access for disadvantaged people. Investigating six diverse local districts, it concluded in 2017 that the current policy was overly focused on new constructions. It recommended a shift to an active management of existing social housing stocks, particularly through increased transparency and a reinforced piloting at the municipal level. As a result, the government launched a housing plan in September 2017 emphasising mobility and transparency besides the construction of new social housing.

- Italy recently undertook a review of its registration processes for food businesses. It compared regulatory arrangements in France, Italy, Spain and the United Kingdom. The review highlighted cases of regulatory overlap and gold-plating. It further noted that some of the information required to be provided to public authorities was obsolete, redundant, unnecessary, or not actually legislatively required. In response to the review, Italy revised its standardised notification requirements in line with practices in other European countries.

- The Netherlands carried out a study comparing regulatory burden for SME's in the bakery sector across selected EU Member States. The evaluation compared the impact of the regulatory frameworks in the Netherlands, Lithuania, Spain and Ireland. The objective was to assess whether significant differences existed in the implementation of national and EU legislation resulting in unnecessary regulatory burdens. The review concluded that the use of exemptions and lighter-touch regulatory regimes for SME bakeries in EU laws could reduce regulatory burdens and improve their economic viability.

- The New Zealand Productivity Commission was asked by the Government to conduct a review of the policy framework for tertiary education and how it might adapt to meet technological, demographic and other challenges. It found that the sector was too constrained by government settings and lacked innovations needed to meet societal needs. Recommendations were made in relation to information to support new models, financing arrangements and regulation, including in relation to quality assurance, access to courses, entry to the sector and the balance between research and teaching.

Source: OECD (2017); (Australian Productivity Commission, 1999[15]), (Australian Productivity Commission, n.d.[16]); (Court of Auditors (France), 2017[17]); (Ministry of Cohesion of Territories and Relations with Local Authorities (France), 2017[18]); (Italy Simplification Project Delivery Unit, 2017[19]); (SIRA Consulting, 2013[20]); (Implementeringsrådet, 2018[21]); (New Zealand Productivity Commission, 2017[22]).

**"Benchmarking" of regulation can be a powerful mechanism for identifying improvements based on comparisons with jurisdictions having similar policy objectives.**

In many cases it can be difficult to determine the "counterfactual" – how things would have turned out under a different regime – in assessing a regulation's performance, particularly where no major problems have arisen. Comparisons of regulatory performance across jurisdictions can be an effective means of gaining insights about the potential benefits to be had from adopting different design features, or alternative instruments. For example, one jurisdiction may choose to adopt performance based approaches to food regulation or workplace safety instead of a prescriptive approach; or impose regulatory barriers to entry to maintain transport quality standards versus a monitoring/complaints regime.

Such comparisons across jurisdictions can also serve as a form of competitive pressure for underperforming jurisdictions to adopt reforms.

A proviso is that the jurisdiction is sufficiently similar institutionally and with respect to its policy goals in the area concerned for the comparisons to have relevance. This requirement would be most closely satisfied in Federal or quasi Federal systems of government.

Based on this logic, a special series of benchmarking reviews were conducted in Australia that compared indicators from several jurisdictions within its Federation (outlined below). There are also some similar international exercises, such as the World Bank "Doing Business" report and, in the education sphere, the OECD's annual PISA survey.

## Ongoing stock management

In many cases, there is potential for "continuous improvement" to regulations in response to information emerging through administrative processes about their operations and effectiveness.

**There need to be mechanisms in place that enable "on the ground" learnings by enforcement bodies about a regulation's performance to be conveyed to relevant areas of government with policy responsibility.**

Regulatory agencies with enforcement powers and inspection authorities are often best placed to ascertain how well a regulation is performing in such key respects as ease of administration and compliance, and achieving behavioural change. They can potentially play an important role in transmitting such information back to those responsible for regulatory design, whether within the regulatory body itself or in an overseeing department or ministry. However, such feedback loops are not well developed in most administrations despite longstanding recognition of the potential benefits (HM Treasury UK, 2005[23]); (OECD, 2017[24]).

It is important therefore to develop internal mechanisms to communicate information about the "real time" performance of regulations in place, as this may avoid the need for larger reviews at a later stage when problems have become more manifest.

**Regulatory offset rules (such as "one-in one-out") and burden reduction targets or quotas, need to include a requirement that regulations slated for removal, if still "active", first undergo some form of assessment as to their worth.**

Formalised stock-flow rules that require the removal of existing regulations when introducing new ones, or that require agencies to reduce "red tape burdens" by certain amounts annually, employ what are effectively simple decision rules to contain aggregate costs of administration and compliance. Such approaches have been widely used across the OECD; see, e.g. (Trnka and Thuerer, 2019[25]). These have often taken the form of annual bundled "clean-up" regulations, and have also been introduced at the subnational levels of government in some countries.

Burden reduction programs and regulatory offsets can act as an important complement to *ex post* reviews. While not strictly forms of evaluation in themselves, they can provide the motivation to evaluate the worth of regulations in place. However it is important that they not be administered bluntly, in a way that focuses more on costs than benefits of regulation. To avoid perverse effects, both sides need to be considered before changes are made.

That said, such assessments need to be proportionate so as not to negate the advantages of one-in-one-out rules in terms of administrative costs. It would be sufficient to be able to conclude that removing the regulation would be likely to yield a net benefit.

## Review methods should themselves be reviewed periodically to ensure that they too remain fit for purpose.

As noted, there are advantages in employing a mix of review types to ensure that nothing "falls between the cracks" and that effort can be distributed according to the significance of different regulations and the potential payoffs from review (Box 2.6). But it is also important that the review techniques are themselves reviewed at intervals to ensure that they are achieving what is intended. For example, a review method that is effective in the early phase of a shift to greater evaluation of regulation may not be so effective when most "low hanging fruit" has been picked. A number of jurisdictions have undertaken such reviews (UK National Audit Office, 2011[26]), (European Court of Auditors, 2018[27]) and some have made significant changes to their *ex post* review systems as a result; see (OECD, 2010[28]) Annex 2.

---

### Box 2.6. The emerging use of behavioural insights

Behavioural insights (BI) builds on lessons derived from the behavioural and social sciences, including decision making, psychology, cognitive science, neuroscience, organisational and group behaviour and is being used by governments around the world to make public policy more effective. BI takes an inductive approach to policy-making that is driven by experimentation and piloting, which challenges established assumptions of what is thought to be rational behaviour of citizens and businesses. While (OECD, 2017[24]) research shows that the majority of the applications of BI to public policy have been to improving the design and implementation of policies, the next frontier is expanding its use to have broader and deeper effects on policymaking.

*Ex post* evaluation present a clear and logical space for expanding the use of the BI methodology. On the one hand, BI is inherently evaluative – experimentation and trialling generates evidence on what works, and what does not, which can be used by policymakers to evaluate the effectiveness of a given policy choice. This is especially powerful when paired up with behaviourally-informed *ex ante* RIAs, where *ex post* evaluation can reflect upon the degree to which a policy decision has met intended outcomes. On the other, BI is a tool for understanding how citizens and businesses actually behave and make decisions. The BI methodology can be applied to evaluating a given policy from a behavioural perspective to discover what, if any, behavioural problems are reducing the effectiveness of the policy choice (OECD, 2019[29]). Policymakers can then use BI to test and implement new policy solutions that better meet intended outcomes.

Source: (OECD, 2017[24]); (OECD, 2019[29]).

---

# References

Australian Office of Best Practice Regulation (2016), *Post-implementation review, Guidance Note*, https://ris.pmc.gov.au/sites/default/files/posts/2016/02/Post-implementation-reviews-guidance-note.pdf.  [8]

Australian Productivity Commission (2011), *Identifying and Evaluating Productivity Commission, Regulation Reforms Research Report*, https://www.pc.gov.au/inquiries/completed/regulation-reforms/report/regulation-reforms.pdf (accessed on 2 July 2020).  [2]

Australian Productivity Commission (2005), *Review of National Competition Policy Reforms: Productivity Commission Inquiry Report No. 33*, https://www.pc.gov.au/inquiries/completed/national-competition-policy/report/ncp.pdf.  [3]

Australian Productivity Commission (1999), *Australia's Gambling Industries*, https://www.pc.gov.au/inquiries/completed/gambling (accessed on 1 July 2020).  [15]

Australian Productivity Commission (n.d.), *Gambling: Inquiry report*, 2010, https://www.pc.gov.au/inquiries/completed/gambling-2010/report (accessed on 1 July 2020).  [16]

Court of Auditors (France) (2017), *The challenge of access to social housing facing modest and disadvantage public*, https://www.ccomptes.fr/fr/publications/le-logement-social-face-au-defi-de-lacces-des-publics-modestes-et-defavorises (accessed on 29 June 2020).  [17]

Danish Business Forum (n.d.), , http://www.enkereregler.dk (accessed October 2018).  [13]

Department of Public Administration Simplification Office (Italy) (2017), *L'agenda per la semplificazione 2015-2017 (The Agenda for Simplification 2015-2017)*, http://www.italiasemplice.gov.it/media/2062/agenda_semplificazione_2015-2017.pdf (accessed on 1 July 2020).  [14]

European Court of Auditors (2018), *Ex-post review of EU legislation: a well-established system, but incomplete, Special Report No. 16*, https://www.eca.europa.eu/lists/ecadocuments/sr18_16/sr_better_regulation_en.pdf (accessed on 29 June 2020).  [27]

HM Treasury UK (2005), *Reducing administrative burdens: effective inspection and enforcement*, http://news.bbc.co.uk/nol/shared/bsp/hi/pdfs/bud05hampton_150305_640.pdf.  [23]

Hungarian Administrative and Justice Ministry (n.d.), *Az új hatásvizsgálati rendszer és hatásvizsgálati lap általános bemutatása (General presentation of the new impact assessment system and impact assessment sheet)*, https://www.vie-publique.fr/sites/default/files/rapport/pdf/174000693.pdf.  [5]

Implementeringsrådet (2018), *Oversigt anbefalinger nabotjek*, https://star.dk/media/6417/oversigt-implementeringsraadets-anbefalinger-og-iu-svar-nabotjek.pdf (accessed October 2018).  [21]

Italy Simplification Project Delivery Unit (2017), *Agenda per la semplificazione 2015-2017, Sesto Rapporto di monitoraggio, (Simplification Agenda 2015-2017, Sixth monitoring report)*, http://www.italiasemplice.gov.it/media/2524/vi-report-di-attuazione-dellagenda-per-la-semplificazione-30112017.pdf.  [19]

Legislation.co.uk (2015), *Small Business, Enterprise and Employment Act 2015*, http://www.legislation.gov.uk/ukpga/2015/26/contents/enacted (accessed on 2 July 2020). [6]

Ministry of Cohesion of Territories and Relations with Local Authorities (France) (2017), *The Government's housing strategy*, https://www.gouvernement.fr/en/the-government-s-housing-strategy (accessed on 1 July 2020). [18]

New Zealand Productivity Commission (2017), *New models of tertiary education*, https://www.productivity.govt.nz/assets/Documents/2d561fce14/Final-report-Tertiary-Education.pdf. [22]

OECD (2019), *Tools and Ethics for Applied Behavioural Insights: The BASIC Toolkit*, OECD Publishing, Paris, https://dx.doi.org/10.1787/9ea76a8f-en. [29]

OECD (2018), *OECD Regulatory Policy Outlook 2018*, OECD Publishing, Paris, https://dx.doi.org/10.1787/9789264303072-en. [4]

OECD (2017), *Behavioural Insights and Public Policy: Lessons from Around the World*, OECD Publishing, Paris, https://dx.doi.org/10.1787/9789264270480-en. [24]

OECD (2016), *OECD Best Practice Principles: Stakeholder Engagement in Regulatory Policy, Draft for public consultation*, OECD, http://dx.doi.org/GOV/RPC/MRP(2016)1/ANN. [12]

OECD (2015), "Ex post evaluation of regulation: An overview of the notion and of international practices", in *Regulatory Policy in Perspective: A Reader's Companion to the OECD Regulatory Policy Outlook 2015*, OECD Publishing, Paris, https://dx.doi.org/10.1787/9789264241800-8-en. [1]

OECD (2015), *OECD Regulatory Policy Outlook 2015*, OECD Publishing, Paris, https://dx.doi.org/10.1787/9789264238770-en. [11]

OECD (2010), *Why Is Administrative Simplification So Complicated?: Looking beyond 2010*, Cutting Red Tape, OECD Publishing, Paris, https://dx.doi.org/10.1787/9789264089754-en. [28]

OECD/KDI (2017), *Improving Regulatory Governance: Trends, Practices and the Way Forward*, OECD Publishing, Paris, https://dx.doi.org/10.1787/9789264280366-en. [7]

PISG Legal Information System (n.d.), *Rules of Procedure of the Government of the Republic of Slovenia*, http://www.pisrs.si/Pis.web/pregledPredpisa?id=POSL32 (accessed on 30 June 2020). [9]

Regulation Taskforce (2006), *Rethinking Regulation: Report of the Taskforce on Reducing Regulatory Burdens on Business*, https://www.pc.gov.au/research/supporting/regulation-taskforce/report/regulation-taskforce2.pdf. [10]

SIRA Consulting (2013), *The CAR-Methodology applied to SME bakeries and a Scoping Comparison of Regulatory Burden in four EU Member States: Final report, study commissioned by the Dutch Ministry of Economic Affairs, Netherlands*. [20]

Trnka, D. and Y. Thuerer (2019), "One-In, X-Out: Regulatory offsetting in selected OECD countries", *OECD Regulatory Policy Working Papers*, No. 11, OECD Publishing, Paris, https://dx.doi.org/10.1787/67d71764-en. [25]

UK National Audit Office (2011), *Delivering regulatory reform*, https://www.nao.org.uk/wp-content/uploads/2011/02/1011758es.pdf. [26]

# 3 Governance of individual reviews

**The governance and resourcing of reviews, and the approaches employed, need to be proportionate to the nature and significance of the regulations concerned. While needing to be cost effective, arrangements should be such as to facilitate findings and recommendations that are sufficiently well supported to be publicly credible.**

While it is important that no regulation escapes scrutiny, evaluations need to be proportionate and fit for purpose. There are a number of dimensions to this, including the scope and depth of a review, as well as the resources employed. Conducting reviews is not a costless exercise. Spending disproportionate time and money on some regulations may leave other necessary reviews under-resourced. Regulations of major significance need to be resourced sufficiently to conduct rigorous analysis and engage in broad consultations.

**For many regulations, evaluations will be most appropriately conducted within the department or ministry having policy responsibility. Enforcement bodies should normally not conduct reviews themselves, but they are uniquely placed to offer relevant information and advice, and should be closely consulted.**

Departments and ministries responsible for regulation have a number of advantages in overseeing *ex post* reviews of regulation, including greater subject knowledge, familiarity with developments over the life of a regulation, the ability to draw on relevant skills and to undertake reviews at relatively low cost.

Regulatory enforcement bodies within a ministry will typically be a key source of performance information, especially about compliance rates and the costs of administering a regulatory regime. It is important that there is systematic provision for harnessing their knowledge. However, principles of good governance require that these bodies not have responsibility for reviewing their own performance, nor for making recommendations about the regulations they must administer and enforce.

**The more "sensitive" a regulation, and the more significant its economic or social impacts, the stronger the case for an "arm's-length" or independent review process. This in turn requires, at a minimum, that those leading a review are not beholden to the agency concerned, and have no perceived conflicts of interest.**

Agencies responsible for regulation, while usually having expert knowledge, can also have mixed incentives when it comes to assessing and reporting on how well a regulation has performed. This can reflect concerns about the prospect of criticism or "blame", or even about potential disruption to the status quo. How much of a problem this is in practice could depend on a variety of things, including staff turnover in relevant roles within a department and whether the government that made a regulation is still in power at the time of it being reviewed.

This is more likely to be an issue where a regulatory area is publicly or politically contentious, with the need to act also being influenced by the impacts of the regulatory regime.

The degree of independence called for will generally be a judgment call. However, at a minimum, the test should be that while the reviewer will need relevant knowledge and experience, there should be no conflicts of interest – real or perceived – or reasons for being unduly influenced by different interests, including from within the policy portfolio. Some countries have used standing bodies from within government to conduct such reviews (with about half the OECD member counties reporting that they have such bodies), and most have used *ad hoc* taskforces or committees of review formed specifically for a review task (Box 3.1).

---

### Box 3.1. Selected independent reviews in OECD countries

- In **Australia**, following public concern about the levels of remuneration of senior executives in public companies, the Productivity Commission was asked to conduct a public inquiry and make recommendations about regulatory or other interventions. The Commission found that on average the trends in remuneration could be justified by company growth and international influences. However, there were instances of excessive payouts and incentives unrelated to performance that suggested a need for better governance and regulation to ensure improved accountability and oversight. Among the recommendations made (and accepted by Government) was the introduction of a "two strikes rule" whereby a company receiving a "no vote" greater than 25% on its remuneration report at two Annual General Meetings, would be obliged to have a vote as to the holding of a special meeting at which the board presented itself for re-election.

- The **Belgian** Court of Auditors recently reviewed the supervision of medical insurance funds and recommended that all parties agree on the scope and implementation of mandatory sickness and invalidity insurance. It also recommended that risk analysis be undertaken based on information provided by mutual societies, and that in light of the additional information available, the selection of domains and indicators, and the definition of scales evaluation criteria be given more attention.

- The **Icelandic** Tourist Board, an independent authority under the Ministry of Industry and Innovation, conducted a public stocktake review of the regulatory framework in tourism in 2014. After extensive consultation with public agencies, local authorities, and industry organisations, the report recommended to simplify the licensing system. The establishment of one-stop shops was forecast to enable private, short-term rentals to be notified to the authorities instead of through licensing arrangements.

- The Law Reform Commission in **Ireland** has a process to identify and select laws to review based on their societal impact. Since its creation in 1975, it has undertaken detailed reviews into numerous areas including marriage, administrative and criminal law, and insurance contracts. It is currently undertaking its Fourth Programme of Law Reform.

- The **New Zealand** Productivity Commission was asked to conduct an independent public inquiry into its "regulatory institutions and practices". The inquiry found that quality checks were "under strain", that much regulation was often out of date or not fit-for-purpose, that there were skill deficits among regulators and inadequacies in the monitoring of their performance. It recommended greater oversight and direction from the centre of government, including in relation to supervision, coordination and prioritization. It also recommended upgrading and clarifying ministerial and central agency responsibilities for ensuring effective regulatory systems and outcomes.

Source: (OECD, 2017[1]); (Australian Productivity Commission, 2009[2]); (Court of Auditors (Belgium), 2018[3]); (Icelandic Tourist Board, 2014[4]); (Law Reform Commission (Ireland), n.d.[5]); (New Zealand Productivity Commission, 2014[6]).

**Transparency is paramount for in-depth reviews. Reviews should be publicly announced, and provide scope for input from stakeholders and the wider public, with findings/recommendations and the response by government both made publicly available.**

For more significant reviews in areas of regulation with major impacts and/or strong community interest, it is important that draft reports be prepared for public discussion and feedback, including on preliminary findings and recommendations (Banks, 2014[7]).

While final review reports should be made publicly available, this need not be prior to a decision being made. However, a government's decision in response to a final report's recommendations (whether acceptance or rejection) should be made and published within a reasonable period and one that has been designated in advance (ideally 2-3 months).

Governments are obviously not obliged to accept a review's recommendations. But when they choose not to do so, the basis for this should be explained to the public. Lack of information about the outcome of past reviews can reduce the future willingness of stakeholders to participate in the process (devoting time and resources to preparing submissions, responding to data requests, etc.) and may erode public trust in government's regulatory efforts generally.

## References

Australian Productivity Commission (2009), *Executive Remuneration in Australia, Productivity Commission Inquiry Report No. 49*, https://www.pc.gov.au/inquiries/completed/executive-remuneration/report/executive-remuneration-report.pdf. [2]

Banks, G. (2014), *Making public policy in the public interest: the role of public inquiries in Royal Commissions and Public Inquiries: Practice and Potential*, Prasser, S. and H. Tracey, Connor Court, Sydney, https://static1.squarespace.com/static/563997f0e4b0d7adb678285e/t/58b76ad5a5790a24a5335014/1488415452353/Making+Public+Policy+in+the+Public+Interest.pdf (accessed on 1 July 2020). [7]

Court of Auditors (Belgium) (2018), *Supervision of the medical insurance funds*, https://www.ccrek.be/EN/Publications/Fiche.html?id=4ebd199f-a9ed-43f2-b132-a4c659f0e022 (accessed on 29 June 2020). [3]

Icelandic Tourist Board (2014), *Einföldun starfs umhverfis og reglu verks í ferðaþjónustu á Íslandi – Tillögur stýrihóps Ferðamálastofu til iðnaðar-og viðskiptaráðherra (Impact of staff requirements and regulatory services in Iceland: Proposals by the Icelandic Tourist Board to the Minister of Industry and Commerce)*, https://www.stjornarradid.is/media/atvinnuvegaraduneyti-media/media/Acrobat/FMS---Einfoldun-starfsumhverfis-og-regluverks-i-ferdathjonustu---Mai-2014.pdf. [4]

Law Reform Commission (Ireland) (n.d.), *Programmes of Law Reform*, https://www.lawreform.ie/law-reform/our-programmes-of-law-reform.127.html (accessed on 30 October 2018). [5]

New Zealand Productivity Commission (2014), *Regulatory institutions and practices*, https://www.productivity.govt.nz/inquiries/regulatory-institutions-and-practices/ (accessed on 1 July 2020). [6]

OECD (2017), *Behavioural Insights and Public Policy: Lessons from Around the World*, OECD Publishing, Paris, https://dx.doi.org/10.1787/9789264270480-en. [1]

# 4 Key questions for reviews

Reviews concerned with the performance of regulation, rather than merely assessing procedural or compliance matters, will generally need to address four key questions.

## Appropriateness: reviews should address as a threshold question whether a valid rationale for regulating still exists.

In assessing the performance of a regulation or regulatory regime, it is important firstly to determine whether the original policy logic justifying it still stands, given changes that may have subsequently occurred in policy frameworks, the economy or society. In cases where the rationale was not made clear at the outset – a not infrequent occurrence – this may require the reviewer to determine what it *should* have been, or at least what it should be going forward.

A commonly cited rationale for regulating comes under the rubric of "market failure", where features inherent to some markets, such as asymmetric information or externalities, can lead to inefficient economic outcomes that may be ameliorated through government intervention. Other legitimate policy rationales include achieving more equitable outcomes (for citizens or regions) than markets would produce, or enhancing opportunities for citizens through better access to basic services such as education and health.

## Effectiveness: reviews should determine whether the regulation (or set of regulations) actually achieves the objectives for which it was introduced.

Regulation is not of value for its own sake. It is (or needs to be) predicated on the expectation of it addressing a policy issue or problem so as to improve things. It is therefore fundamental in reviewing the performance of regulations in place that outcomes in the policy area of concern are assessed relative to what otherwise would have occurred. That is not to suggest that this is easy to achieve, given that there will often be multiple influences on observed outcomes over time, but without this as the objective, it will be harder to identify enhancements and build public confidence in regulation itself.

## Efficiency: reviews need to determine whether regulations give rise to unnecessary costs (beyond those needed to achieve the policy goal) or have other unintended impacts.

The overall benefits to society of regulation need to account not only for its effectiveness in addressing a public policy issue, but also the costs and other impacts incurred in doing so (OECD, 2012[1]). Improved outcomes in a particular domain, for example reduced city congestion, may not be worth having if the cost of achieving these leads to worse outcomes elsewhere. A good regulation would achieve its goal at minimum cost and without leading to unintended adverse outcomes as a side effect.

**Alternatives: reviews should consider whether modifications to regulations, or their replacement by alternative policy instruments, are called for.**

An *ex post* review is of little value if it does not either affirm that a regulation is performing well and needs no change, or identify changes that would improve its performance. It is thus important that reviews be required to make recommendations about any changes considered beneficial. Consideration also needs to be given to how recommendations can be most effectively put into effect.

## Reference

OECD (2012), *Recommendation of the Council on Regulatory Policy and Governance*, OECD Publishing, Paris, https://www.oecd.org/governance/regulatory-policy/49990817.pdf.　　　　[1]

# 5 Methodologies

In seeking to answer these basic questions, a review would need to shine light on a variety of further issues. For example: How well were the regulations administered? To what extent did they bring about changes in behaviour? How were impacts distributed across the community?

Unlike *ex ante* assessments, the ability exists to consider information relating to *actual* impacts of the regulations under review. Answering such questions is rarely straightforward and efforts would need to be proportionate to the significance of the regulations concerned. They can be assisted by adopting a systematic approach that includes the following features.

## Evaluations of regulations should be conducted within a "cost-benefit" framework that firstly identifies and documents impacts of relevance, and then assesses their relative magnitude.

Most regulations will have a variety of impacts of varying significance. These can be economic, social or environmental. Impacts can also vary within the community and across regions within a country. Such impacts need to be identified in a systematic way as a precursor to the more difficult task of assessing the net effects (see Box 5.1). The enumeration of different impacts can in itself often provide useful insights.

Where feasible, indirect as well as direct effects need to be accounted for. Impacts on parties not targeted by the regulation, or "downstream" from those who are, can sometimes outweigh the direct impacts. For example, a regulation that imposes requirements on producers to meet certain desirable environmental objectives, may involve significant costs being passed on to other producers, which can work against a government's economic development objectives. And rules that impact on prices or market competition can have impacts on innovation and productivity.

---

**Box 5.1. Cost-benefit analysis of regulation**

As its name suggests, cost-benefit analysis (CBA) is a method of evaluating the worth of a regulatory (or spending) initiative based on a systematic appraisal of both its costs and benefits. It had its origins in defence spending decision-making in the United States in the 1950s, but has been developed and extended greatly since then, including as a key part of *ex ante* and *ex post* reviews of regulation in many countries.

In principle, CBA involves quantifying in monetary terms the present value of all the costs and benefits of a proposal, so that a clear conclusion can be drawn as to its net value to society. Thus, a regulatory initiative for which the estimated benefits were less than the costs would not normally proceed.

However when it comes to regulation, particularly in the social and environmental domains, not everything can be confidently valued. This means that what can be done in a CBA in practice will often fall short of the ideal. Nevertheless, the CBA framework remains a valuable tool for regulatory assessment. The systematic identification of costs and benefits, which is the first step in CBA, can in

---

itself be a useful discipline and an antidote to the tendency to focus on the benefits of a regulation. And to the extent that the cost side can be more readily quantified in monetary terms than the benefits side, insights can be gained as to how great the benefits would need to be to justify proceeding.

The steps that need to be taken in CBA are similar to those that apply to a regulation impact assessment. The key ones are:

- Identify the options to be compared. Ideally there should be more than one, as a CBA may be positive in one case but larger in another.
- Identify the range of costs and benefits, which should be incremental to "business as usual".
- Monetise where feasible and do so over the life of the proposal, discounting to a common present value.
- Undertake "sensitivity analysis" to see how changes in individual assumptions or estimates affect the results.

Key issues along the way include valuation methods and choice of discount rate. A number of governments provide guidance or "rules" about these, and agencies can call on specialists in the field of CBA and evaluation from among consulting organisations and academia. Experience suggests that while quantification can be challenging, there is much that can be achieved, including through special purpose data collections and surveys where the topic is of sufficient importance to warrant the time and effort. Examples of methodologies include "revealed" and "stated preferences", and "secondary source" valuations, as well as "triangulation" techniques. (An example of innovative approaches to quantification can be found in the Australian Productivity Commission's reports on gambling regulation (Australian Productivity Commission, 1999[1]); (Australian Productivity Commission, n.d.[2]).

Source: (Australian Office of Best Practice Regulation, 2020[3]).

## Quantification should be attempted where feasible and cost effective, as it can bring additional rigour to assessments of impacts and potential outcomes.

Evaluations typically need to draw on both qualitative and quantitative methods of analysis. In many cases, the qualitative considerations will be among the more important (e.g. environmental amenity, perceptions of safety, etc.). However, the greater the quantification of impacts, the easier it will generally be to make an overall assessment where subjective elements are present.

An estimate of costs expressed in money terms will often help in making judgments as to whether benefits that cannot be so expressed are "worth it". For example, would the amenity value of retaining heritage features of the built environment in a potential industry development area outweigh the estimated income gains from change of use? Would preservation of native fauna be worth the estimated costs of restricting agricultural development? An ability to pose such questions can help inform necessary value judgments at the political level.

More refined quantitative methods such as multivariate or regression analysis can also provide a rigorous means of determining *causality*; that is, for distinguishing impacts due to a regulatory intervention from those potentially attributable to other changes or influences; see (Malyshev, 2006[4]); (OECD, 2011[5]).

## Data requirements are best considered at the time a regulation is being made, as part of wider consideration of the type of *ex post* review that would be most appropriate.

Reviews can fail to produce credible findings and recommendations for lack of adequate 'evidence'. Standard data collections within government may not have the granularity or specificity needed to evaluate all relevant impacts of a regulation. In such circumstances it may be that the data needed to assess performance has to be collected as part of the regulatory regime itself. This can be done under compliance reporting obligations and/or through survey instruments. If the latter, the usual precautions against response bias apply.

Regulated entities will generally be a useful source of qualitative information, but should be encouraged to provide quantitative evidence as well. Administrative data sources are increasingly being used in the quantification of impacts; see (Crato and Paruolo, 2019[6]).

The increasing availability of open data, "big data" and new statistical techniques have considerable potential both to enhance evaluations and enable innovations in how these are conducted. Patterns and responses may be discernible that would not have been possible using traditional statistical methods. This is a relatively new area and one that holds out considerable scope for learning across jurisdictions.

## The observed impacts of a regulation should ideally be compared with "counterfactuals" – how things would have turned out otherwise.

At issue in a regulatory review is not just whether a given regulatory regime has on balance achieved its goal or yielded certain benefits, but whether better results may be achievable in future by adopting modifications or using alternative policy instruments, or indeed without further government intervention at all. In this sense an *ex post* review must also involve some *ex ante* analysis. The difference in this case is that actual data on impacts to date should be available. This can provide a more tractable foundation for analysing how variations could have made a difference in the past.

As noted previously, one useful technique for understanding "counterfactuals" is to benchmark domestic regulations against those found in other jurisdictions that address the same policy issue using alternative approaches. As also noted, the most useful jurisdictions for benchmarking purposes will be those where the policy objectives and broad institutional structures are similar to those domestically. It is a technique well-suited to federal systems of government, therefore, as well as at the local government level (Box 5.2).

---

### Box 5.2. Selected OECD benchmarking reviews

- In Australia, the Council of Australian Governments agreed in 2006 to adopt a common framework for benchmarking, measuring and reporting the regulatory burdens on business. Following an initial feasibility study, the Productivity Commission was requested to undertake benchmarking studies in the areas of (Australian Productivity Commission, 2010[7]); (Australian Productivity Commission, 2011[8]); (Australian Productivity Commission, 2012[9]); (Australian Productivity Commission, 2012[10]); (Australian Productivity Commission, 2013[11]). Each of these reviews found significant disparities in performance across jurisdictions and made a range of recommendations to bring each up to what was judged to be best practice.

- In 2017, the General Inspection of the Administration in France undertook a review of the outcomes from two recent laws modernising territorial public administration. It found that local actors had not yet fully integrated the public policy tools provided by the laws, in part because of the cumbersome procedure itself, but also an impression by territorial administrations of being under a trusteeship model and that the model was a hindrance to proper competence transfer from the State to local actors or among local actors themselves. Nevertheless, the reforms initiated new territorial cooperation with an increasing focus on structural strategy and competence issues rather than on particular, contractual projects, which have the potential to improve administrative efficacy. The report made a series of recommendations including to improve the cooperative environment so as to better facilitate synergies between Departments

---

and Metropoles on social policies, as well as to take better account of the needs of local public service users in the competence re-organisation process.

- While still the National Commission for Regulatory Improvement in Mexico (CONAMER) undertook a review of regulatory simplification processes for new low-risk start-up businesses in representative municipalities from five states. It was found that the programme of regulatory simplification had not only led to a substantive reduction in turnaround times, but that the number of entrepreneurs in the municipalities rose significantly.

Source: (OECD, 2017[12]); (Australian Productivity Commission, 2010[7]); (Australian Productivity Commission, 2011[8]); (Australian Productivity Commission, 2012[9]); (Australian Productivity Commission, 2012[10]); (Australian Productivity Commission, 2013[11]); (General Inspection of the Administration (France), 2017[13]); (National Commission for Regulatory Improvement (CONAMER), 2019[14]).

# References

Australian Office of Best Practice Regulation (2020), *Cost-benefit analysis guidance note*, https://www.pmc.gov.au/sites/default/files/publications/cost-benefit-analysis_0.pdf (accessed on 2 July 2020). [3]

Australian Productivity Commission (2013), *Regulator Engagement with Small Business, Research Report, Canberra*, https://www.pc.gov.au/inquiries/completed/small-business/report/small-business.pdf. [11]

Australian Productivity Commission (2012), *Performance Benchmarking of Australian Business Regulation: The Role of Local Government as Regulator, Research Report, Canberra*, https://www.pc.gov.au/inquiries/completed/regulation-benchmarking-local-government/report. [9]

Australian Productivity Commission (2012), *Regulatory Impact Analysis: Benchmarking, Research Report, Canberra*, https://www.pc.gov.au/inquiries/completed/regulatory-impact-analysis-benchmarking/report/ria-benchmarking.pdf. [10]

Australian Productivity Commission (2011), *Performance Benchmarking of Australian Business Regulation: Planning, Zoning and Development Assessment, Research Report, Canberra*, https://www.pc.gov.au/inquiries/completed/regulation-benchmarking-planning/report. [8]

Australian Productivity Commission (2010), *Performance Benchmarking of Australian Business Regulation: Occupational Health & Safety, Research Report, Canberra*, https://www.pc.gov.au/inquiries/completed/regulation-benchmarking-ohs/report/ohs-report.pdf. [7]

Australian Productivity Commission (1999), *Australia's Gambling Industries*, https://www.pc.gov.au/inquiries/completed/gambling (accessed on 1 July 2020). [1]

Australian Productivity Commission (n.d.), *Gambling: Inquiry report*, 2010, https://www.pc.gov.au/inquiries/completed/gambling-2010/report (accessed on 1 July 2020). [2]

Crato, N. and P. Paruolo (eds.) (2019), *Data-Driven Policy Impact Evaluation*, Springer International Publishing, Cham, http://dx.doi.org/10.1007/978-3-319-78461-8. [6]

General Inspection of the Administration (France) (2017), *Délégation de compétences et conférence territoriale d'action publique, de nouveaux outils au service de la coopération territoriale*, https://www.vie-publique.fr/sites/default/files/rapport/pdf/174000693.pdf (accessed on 29 October 2018). [13]

Malyshev, N. (2006), "Regulatory Policy: OECD Experience and Evidence", *Oxford Review of Economic Policy*, Vol. 22/2, pp. 274-299, http://dx.doi.org/10.1093/oxrep/grj017. [4]

National Commission for Regulatory Improvement (CONAMER) (2019), *Sistema de Apertura Rápida de Empresas (SARE)*, https://www.gob.mx/conamer/documentos/sistema-de-apertura-rapida-de-empresas-sare (accessed on 2 July 2020). [14]

OECD (2017), *Behavioural Insights and Public Policy: Lessons from Around the World*, OECD Publishing, Paris, https://dx.doi.org/10.1787/9789264270480-en. [12]

OECD (2011), *Regulatory Policy and Governance: Supporting Economic Growth and Serving the Public Interest*, OECD Publishing, Paris, https://dx.doi.org/10.1787/9789264116573-en. [5]

# 6 Public consultation

In some cases, there will be little published information relating to a regulation's operations and impacts, such that reviewers may have to rely entirely on input from stakeholders. However consultation processes can bring other benefits as well and should be provided for as a matter of course.

**All reviews should involve consultations with affected parties and, to the extent possible, be accessible to civil society.**

Since the function of an *ex post* review is to evaluate how well a regulation has been performing in practice, it is important to consult at first hand with those directly affected. Also, engaging with civil society more generally can help to balance concerns raised about costs of regulation with a better appreciation of their wider benefits to society.

Reviews benefit from public/stakeholder participation in a number of ways.

- First, and most obviously, they provide a means of obtaining *more complete information* about impacts and responses, as well as the opportunity to test preliminary analysis and findings.

- Second, engaging stakeholders can help with targeting reviews at regulations or regulatory areas that might be problematic; namely, those that are the most burdensome or irritating for regulated subjects (e.g. the Red Tape Challenge). Likewise, mechanisms that enable more continuous engagement with stakeholders (e.g. the Danish Business Forum) can help identify problematic issues in a timely way.

- Third, in giving the public the opportunity to express views and make an input to proceedings, it can build trust in the review process and even a sense of "ownership' of the outcomes, making the implementation of any changes politically easier to manage than might otherwise have been the case. This is especially important for more sensitive or contentious areas of regulation.

**The nature and coverage of consultations should be proportionate to the significance of the regulations and the degree of public interest or sensitivity entailed.**

Consultations, done well, can be time-consuming and resource intensive. Given budgetary constraints, they need to be conducted in a manner that elicits necessary information at least cost (for a summary of current practices see Box 6.1).

This has implications for both the breadth and depth of consultation activity. Highly technical or complex regulatory areas (e.g. foreign trade regulations) or those with narrow impacts (e.g. related to a particular region) would permit more selectivity in consultation, for example, than regulatory regimes of wider public interest and impact.

More contentious areas of regulation, such as in relation to welfare entitlements or migration or taxation, may require formal proceedings and maximum transparency if they are to satisfy stakeholder expectations and achieve the political benefits noted.

## Box 6.1. Consultation practices across OECD countries

Most OECD countries have enhanced their regulatory consultation practices over recent years. There are now requirements in over 80% of member countries to undertake public consultations on all regulatory proposals. Around 60% of countries publish advance lists of regulations to be prepared, modified, reformed or repealed. This helps to notify interested parties of forthcoming consultations, allowing for a better dialogue between stakeholders and policymakers. OECD member countries regularly publish information received as part of consultations, and views are often summarised in regulatory impact statements.

Nearly two-thirds of member countries now have minimum consultation periods in place so as to facilitate better engagement with affected parties. Likewise, electronic means of communication have become more commonplace, making it easier for stakeholders to provide input to decision makers.

That said, as shown below, the extent of consultation is generally greater in the later than earlier stages of regulatory development.

### Figure 6.1. Consultation undertaken at earlier and later stages of policy development

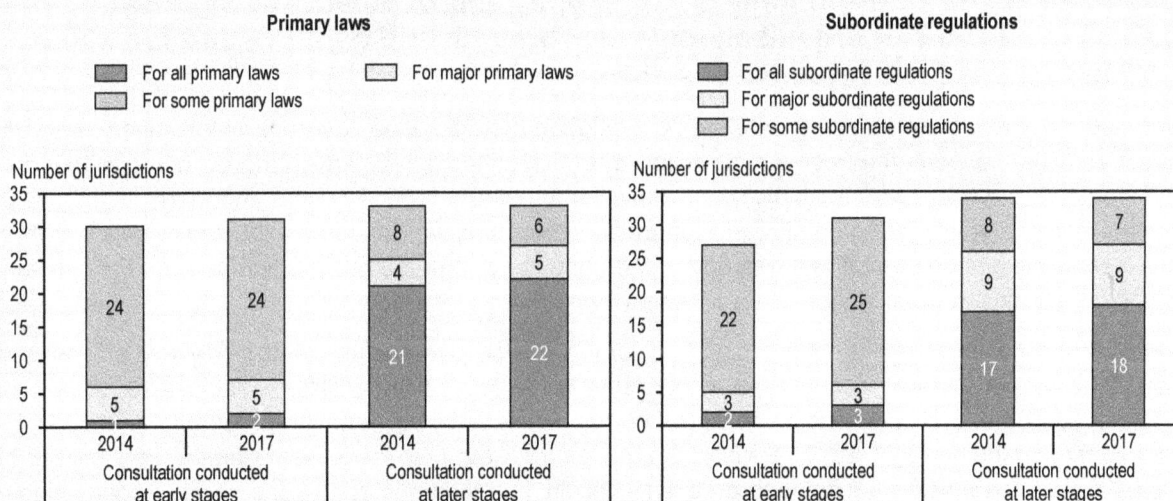

Note: Data is based on 34 OECD member countries and the European Union.
Source: (OECD, 2018[1]), Figure 2.9, https://dx.doi.org/10.1787/9789264303072-en.

## Reference

OECD (2018), *OECD Regulatory Policy Outlook 2018*, OECD Publishing, [1]
Paris, https://dx.doi.org/10.1787/9789264303072-en.

# 7 Prioritisation and sequencing

Apart from the "programmed" and "managerial" review mechanisms, the timing of which will largely be pre-determined, opportunities can usefully be taken to conduct other reviews on an *ad hoc* basis. Indeed some of the largest gains from reform have resulted from such *ad hoc* initiatives (OECD, 2011[1]). That said, given limitations on financial resources and the availability of people with the necessary skills – as well as a need to avoid "review fatigue" – it is important that any such reviews be carefully chosen and sequenced to maximise benefits over time.

**High priority should be given to reviewing regulations that have a) wide application across the economy or community and b) potentially significant impacts on citizens or organisations – i.e. "breadth and depth" – and for which there is c) prima facie evidence of a "problem".**

The three criteria need to be jointly satisfied. A regulation that had wide coverage but involved very little impact, may not be worth the trouble of a review, or at least should have lower priority than one that had both breadth of coverage and depth of impact. However the third criterion is just as important, as the payoff from reviewing even a major area of regulation that is performing well could be expected to be lower than for a less significant one that is not. Moreover, the absence of a perceived problem would likely make it hard to obtain "buy-in" from stakeholders or the public.

Evidence of regulatory failings (undue costs, distortion of incentives, unintended third-party effects) can usefully be obtained pro-actively via surveys or other consultative mechanisms (a "stocktake" review for example) as well as in response to complaints that may be made by those affected. (Examples include the UK Red Tape Challenge, Korea's "Petition Drum" reforms, etc.) However some preliminary testing or vetting of such feedback is desirable to assess its validity and thus ensure that the costs of conducting a review would be warranted.

**Attention to sequencing is important to maximise the realised gains from reform.**

Since the outcome of prioritisation exercises rarely involve much precision, more than one area of regulation will typically have comparable claims. It will commonly not be feasible to review all of these at once and thus other criteria need to come into play.

One relates to any connections between the regulatory areas concerned that could provide a logical reason for doing some before others. For example, a regulation may have effects downstream that relate to other areas of regulation. Normally in such cases it would be preferable to review "up stream" arrangements first. The regulation of producers versus consumers of energy is a topical example. Regulations designed to reduce carbon emissions can be directed at either and typically do both. However requirements affecting production may obviate a need to separately regulate consumption.

Secondly, there will be advantages in choosing a sequence of reviews that takes into account the relative difficulty of implementing identified reforms. This could result from complexity, disruption during the transition or (more commonly) political opposition. The expected payoff from different review exercises would obviously differ where the prospect of obtaining necessary political support differs, even if the substantive gains to be had from reforms were identical in each case.

Thus proceeding in areas that face less political opposition or other implementation challenges makes pragmatic sense. That said, reviews should not be chosen solely according to this criterion, as this could miss areas of greatest potential benefit. The opposition to reform may be overestimated, and in any case it can often be reduced by the review process itself, to the extent that it demonstrates convincingly the gains on offer (OECD, 2010[2]). An example of this is the review into private health insurance regulation conducted by the Industry Commission in Australia in 1997. It found that while the principal of "community rating" – that ensures no discrimination of fees or access based on risk factors – had strong support, in its then form it was leading to "adverse selection" and inequities. These justified amending it to provide for a "loading" on the price of cover for those who defer joining that rises with age of entry. While the Government had previously expressed support for the status quo, it ended up changing the regulatory framework as the review had proposed.

## There are benefits in reviewing regulations as a group, rather than singly, where the regulations concerned are interactive or operate jointly to achieve related policy objectives.

The object of *ex post* reviews is to determine whether changes to a regulation would achieve better outcomes. Where more than one regulation is involved, and overall outcomes are jointly determined, the regulatory regime will generally need to be reviewed as a whole (Box 7.1). Otherwise changes made to parts of a regulatory system may interact with other parts of the system in ways that detract from the intended outcomes. By the same token, if a policy regime contains a mix of regulation and other policy instruments (such as financial transfers) it may be necessary to undertake a wider policy review.

---

### Box 7.1. Selected "packaged" reviews in OECD countries

- The **Canadian** Parliament recently reviewed its commercial vessel length and licensing policies. Regulations relating to fisheries are part of both federal and provincial regulatory competencies. It found that the regulatory framework is complex with differing rules depending on the region fished, with a large regulatory network of responsibilities between the fisheries and transport ministries. A series of recommendations were made to eliminate regulatory inconsistencies in vessel policies across Atlantic Canada, as well as to improve stakeholder consultation with affected parties.

- **Estonia** conducted an economy-wide review of its competitiveness in 2015. Under the supervision of the Ministry of Justice, a Steering Group including different ministries, companies, and associations presented 64 recommendations to government to increase the competitiveness of Estonia's business environment. There was a particularly strong focus on working conditions, contemporary tax issues, reducing administrative burdens, and creating an entrepreneur-friendly legal framework. Those recommendations were incorporated into the Estonia 2020 national reform programme.

- In **New Zealand** a review of local government regulation by the NZ Productivity Commission looked at the overall regulatory performance of local government, including processes and roles. The approach recognised that key elements of the regulatory system are interconnected. It identified some thirty pieces of primary legislation that confer regulatory responsibilities on local government in a more rapidly evolving environment. It found that business saw local regulation as a significant cost burden, with inconsistency of treatment across local government areas a key issue. Recommendations were made in the areas of clarifying roles, strengthening institutions involved in regulation development and enforcement, and improving performance reporting and quality assurance processes.

---

> - The **Swiss** State Secretariat for Economic Affairs conducted a series of reviews based on the impact that digitalisation will have on the Swiss economy. Reports focused on the themes of: the labour market, research and development, the sharing economy, digital finance, and competition policy. One of the reports into the labour market identified that Switzerland is relatively well placed to face the risks associated with employment displacement due to digitalisation, although it was too early to make a conclusive assessment. The report also highlighted the labour market opportunities that might arise as a result of digitalisation and recommended that action be taken to improve data collection relating to new forms of work and that a review of the flexibility of social insurance law be undertaken.
>
> Source: (OECD, 2017[3]); (House of Commons (Canada), 2018[4]); (Estonian Government, 2015[5]); (New Zealand Productivity Commission, 2013[6]); (State Secretariat for Economic Affairs (Switzerland), 2018[7]).

## References

Estonian Government (2015), *Competitiveness 2.0: Report on proposals for increasing the competitiveness of the Estonian business environment*, https://www.eestipank.ee/publikatsioon/eesti-konkurentsivoime-ulevaade/2015/eesti-konkurentsivoime-. [5]

House of Commons (Canada) (2018), *Atlantic Canada's Marine Commercial Vessel Length And Licensing Policies – Working Towards Equitable Policies for Fishers in all of Atlantic Canada, Report of the Standing Committee on Fisheries and Oceans*, http://www.ourcommons.ca (accessed on 29 November 2018). [4]

New Zealand Productivity Commission (2013), *Towards better local regulation*, https://www.productivity.govt.nz/inquiries/towards-better-local-regulation/ (accessed on 1 July 2020). [6]

OECD (2017), *Behavioural Insights and Public Policy: Lessons from Around the World*, OECD Publishing, Paris, https://dx.doi.org/10.1787/9789264270480-en. [3]

OECD (2011), *Regulatory Policy and Governance: Supporting Economic Growth and Serving the Public Interest*, OECD Publishing, Paris, https://dx.doi.org/10.1787/9789264116573-en. [1]

OECD (2010), *Why Is Administrative Simplification So Complicated?: Looking beyond 2010*, Cutting Red Tape, OECD Publishing, Paris, https://dx.doi.org/10.1787/9789264089754-en. [2]

State Secretariat for Economic Affairs (Switzerland) (2018), *Digital economy*, https://www.seco.admin.ch/seco/fr/home/wirtschaftslage---wirtschaftspolitik/wirschaftspolitik/digitalisierung.html (accessed on 29 October 2018). [7]

# 8 Capacity building

**Having in-house capability in evaluation and review methods is essential, both in order to conduct reviews internally as well as to oversee those commissioned externally.**

The goal for public administrators should be to develop and maintain sufficient expertise in evaluation to enable collaborative internal analysis and intelligent external commissioning. This will normally require a "critical mass" of analysts who can work together and learn from each other, and hence help develop a culture of evaluation.

This need not involve special resourcing, as the skill sets relevant to *ex post* assessment of regulations are largely the same as those required for *ex ante* evaluation or RIA processes.

**Capacity enhancement needs to be pursued through training of existing staff as well as through recruitment, with on-the-job learning an important element.**

Some training in evaluation methods is useful for most staff members involved in policy or regulatory areas, since it can enhance their ability to identify and take into account various impacts and help avoid unintended consequences. It can also help build a culture of evaluation, which is conducive to evidence-based policy making generally. Such training can be imparted through special courses, or "on-the-job', which can have the benefit of greater perceived relevance. For example, the Australia and New Zealand School of Government places emphasis on evaluation in its Executive Masters of Public Administration course and offers member governments special training modules in evaluation methods, and cost-benefit analysis in particular.

When capacity needs to be built up from scratch, recruitment of people who are already skilled in evaluation techniques has an obvious role to play. Such recruits can bring the further benefit of imparting knowledge to other staff.

An important complement is ensuring that guidance and training manuals are systematically updated to ensure that staff receive up-to-date training.

**Consultants can usefully supplement expertise available within government, but how they may best contribute in specific cases needs to be carefully considered and they should not be over utilised to the detriment of internal capability.**

External consultants, whether academics or specialist businesses, can usefully supplement government expertise where departments are responsible for reviews, particularly when specialised skills are called for (such as in quantitative analysis or survey design and management).

However, consultants should not be relied on to the point of degrading internal evaluation capacity. Certain reviews will generally need to be conducted internally (e.g. because of political or strategic requirements) and, as noted, it is vital for administrations to retain an ability to quality control externally commissioned work. On this and related issues see (Banks, 2009[1]).

# Reference

Banks, G. (2009), *Evidence-based policy making: What is it? How do we get it?*, Productivity Commission, https://www.pc.gov.au/news-media/speeches/cs20090204/20090204-evidence-based-policy.pdf (accessed on 1 July 2020).     [1]

# 9 Committed leadership

Installing and maintaining regulatory systems consistent with the above principles involves a number of administrative and political challenges. These are more likely to be overcome if governments, and political leaders in particular, demonstrate a commitment to evidence-based policymaking.

Initiatives to reduce red tape and improve regulatory quality are often introduced with good intentions, but commitment to good practices can wane over time. Regulatory disciplines, even when self-imposed, can also be sorely tested by "events" (such as occurred during the financial crisis).

Leadership is instrumental not only in establishing the systems needed to secure regulatory quality, but also for their effective operation over time (OECD, 2012[1]). Such arrangements are intended to limit regulatory freedom of action in the interest of securing better outcomes overall. It is natural that there will be some resistance to this, either at the political or bureaucratic levels. Strong leadership is needed not only to overcome such resistance but also to achieve broad acceptance and endorsement.

## Support from political leaders is essential to the establishment and ongoing effectiveness of systems for the *ex post* review of regulation.

The reality is that *ex post* reviews inform a government's decisions about regulation, rather than supplanting or pre-empting them. While, as noted, such systems necessarily limit freedom of action initially, the findings and recommendations of reviews ultimately have to be agreed to at a political level.

Most regulations involve an element of experimentation. And as noted many face some opposition. Performed well, regulatory reviews not only help governments determine whether regulatory initiatives have turned out as intended, but where changes are needed can help ameliorate the politics. For one thing, as argued previously, to the extent that unintended policy consequences are avoided, this will obviously mean avoiding the political problems that may result, which can be considerable.

But the political environment can also be improved in other ways. Credible assurance from government that proposed regulations will be reviewed after they are implemented can lessen resistance to them. Further, if reviews are conducted through processes that entail significant public participation, stakeholders may develop a sense of ownership of the review and thus of regulatory changes that may result from it.

A "litmus test" for any system of rules is how well it responds to "force majeure". It is inevitable that there will be situations in which exemptions are sought from best practice regulatory requirements. There are benefits in having high-level gatekeeping to vet such claims, as well as to ensure that reviews will be conducted at a subsequent stage.

Governments are not able to bind the actions of their successors, so bipartisan support for regulatory policy is highly desirable if good practice is to be sustained. This requires agreement among political leaders of different parties that, while policy ideas will always be contested, the core elements of good regulatory process will not. This is demonstrated by the continuity observed in many countries following a change in government. It is incumbent on government leaders to seek to secure such agreement, for which purpose consultation (if not collaboration) will generally be required.

**Senior officials within the bureaucracy need to promote a culture of evaluation in their organisations and be vigilant in ensuring that good practice is actually followed "on the ground".**

While a bureaucracy must take its lead from the government of the day, the extent to which regulatory quality systems are upheld and maintained *in practice* crucially depends on its own leadership.

It is one thing to agree on certain best practice principles; it can be another to ensure they are implemented as intended. Just as *ex ante* assessments have often been found deficient, or to have merely provided "backfill" for decisions already taken, *ex post* reviews may be conducted poorly or, worse, arranged such as to provide support for a preordained position. And there is the ever-present risk of a "tick a box" approach to compliance emerging over time, in which form takes precedence over substance.

Such problems have been detected at various times in most jurisdictions. Averting them requires demonstrated commitment by public sector leaders to upholding good process. "Tone at the top" is widely recognised as one of the key influences on the culture within an organisation, which is a primary influence on behaviour.

It needs to be made clear that practices promoting regulatory quality, including *ex post* reviews, are integral to the department's policy functions. Staff need to see the requirements as part of the job, rather than as an imposition. Active support by senior officials for staff training and the recruitment of suitably skilled people is important to this. The establishment of dedicated evaluation units within a department or ministry can provide further tangible evidence. Such units need to be treated as integral to the organisation's purpose, however, rather than simply being about external compliance.

Senior officials play a key role in advising ministers on a range of policy and administrative matters. These need to include guidance about the procedural requirements for making and reviewing regulation. This can be particularly important when a minister is newly appointed, especially if part of a new government that lacks recent experience in office. And if situations arise where there is a wish to circumvent the rules, it can fall on senior officials to "speak truth to power".

These responsibilities are best seen as part of the bureaucracy's wider "stewardship" role over administrative systems and procedures. Such responsibilities should transcend particular government administrations. The institutional memory needed to assure system performance and continuity resides mainly within the bureaucracy, and its leaders are well placed to instruct ministers about best practice requirements, while being responsive to a government's policy agenda.

## Reference

OECD (2012), *Recommendation of the Council on Regulatory Policy and Governance*, OECD Publishing, Paris, https://www.oecd.org/governance/regulatory-policy/49990817.pdf.    [1]